To Bruce, Dan, and Jay

Acknowledgments

Many people helped shape and inform this book.

I'm grateful to Robb Clouse, Solution Tree publisher, for encouraging me to pursue this project and connecting me with his capable team to bring it to life. Thanks to copy editor Rachel Rosolina for her improvements to the manuscript.

A number of busy educators made time for site visits and conversations. Special thanks to Superintendent Pam Moran and her talented crew at Albemarle County Public Schools. Becky Fisher was especially helpful in arranging classroom visits and unpacking her own good thinking. Thanks also to Chad Ratliff, Paula White (and her articulate students), Chad Sansing, Michael Thornton, and many others who are bringing innovation to schools across the district. Dr. Glen Bull and his team at University of Virginia were similarly generous with their time and ideas about children's engineering.

Chris Lehmann and his staff and students at Science Leadership Academy are demonstrating that we don't have to wait to start innovating in education. They do it every day. By hosting EduCon, they bring a much broader audience into conversations about the future of teaching and learning. Thanks to SLA for leading by example and being a catalyst for change.

I'm grateful to Deborah Parizek and her colleagues at the Henry Ford Learning Institute for allowing me to join them in Detroit, Michigan, for an enlightening "deep dive" into design thinking. Thanks, too, to Rich Crandall and his colleagues from the Stanford d.school K–12 Laboratory.

Jonathan Martin is an educational leader with an infectious passion for innovation. Thanks for the invitation to St. Gregory College Preparatory School, where I had the pleasure of watching young innovators at work in Dennis Conner's Design/Build Lab.

Many teachers helped by sharing the stories behind their inspiring projects, including Emily Pilloton, Mike Town, Antero Garcia, Michael Baer, and more. Hat tip to you all for the innovative work you do with students. Thanks, too, to colleague Jane Krauss for being an excellent sounding board.

To my friends at Edutopia, thanks for creating a platform for showcasing the work of inspiring educators and a network for helping grow good ideas.

I've had the privilege of learning about innovation from many who are tackling difficult problems in communities around the world. Thanks to all these wonderfully unreasonable people who are working tirelessly to create a better future. You are offering today's students some excellent footprints to follow.

Finally, thanks to my husband, Bruce Rubin, for your always helpful feedback, good humor, and unflagging encouragement.

Solution Tree Press would like to thank the following reviewers:

Jeanne Black
Instructional Facilitator
East Middle School
Biscoe, North Carolina

Francesca Branson
English Department Chair and
    AP Literature Teacher
James Madison High School
Vienna, Virginia

Dennis Conner
Physics and Computer Science
    Teacher
St. Gregory College Preparatory
    School
Tucson, Arizona

Lyn Hilt
Principal
Brecknock Elementary School
Denver, Pennsylvania

Amy Nicodemus
Chemistry Teacher
Barrington High School
Barrington, Rhode Island

Barbara Williams
Social Studies Department Chair
Buena High School
Sierra Vista, Arizona

Table of Contents

About the Author

Suzie Boss is a writer and educational consultant who focuses on the power of teaching and learning to improve lives and transform communities. Coauthor of *Reinventing Project-Based Learning: Your Field Guide to Real-World Projects in the Digital Age*, she is a regular contributor to *Edutopia* and the *Stanford Social Innovation Review*. Her writing has appeared in a wide range of other publications, including *Educational Leadership*, *Principal Leadership*, *The New York Times*, and *Huffington Post*. She is on the National Faculty of the Buck Institute for Education and has worked with educators internationally to bring project-based learning to both traditional classrooms and informal learning settings. Collaborating with nonprofit organizations, she has helped develop programs that engage youth and adults as innovative community problem solvers.

Foreword

Suzie Boss occupies three worlds, all of which are powerfully on display in *Bringing Innovation to School*. First, Suzie is a first-rate journalist; she has the ability to weave a story together with a fresh lens that always leaves me learning from her writing.

And that's a second world; although she may not always accept the mantle, Suzie is a profound teacher. Through the many conversations I have had with Suzie, the times I have gone to one of her workshops, and the times I have read her work, I have learned greatly from her. As a result, the Science Leadership Academy—the funky little school that a group of amazing teachers and I started in Philadelphia—is far better off for our institutional friendship with Suzie.

As both a journalist and a teacher, Suzie inhabits a third space that perhaps eclipses both of those roles. Suzie is a habitual learner, and her joy for learning is infectious. Suzie is the kind of person who leans in during a conversation with you. She has a way of making you feel like your conversation is the most important conversation she could be having at that moment. And I cannot recall a conversation I have had with Suzie that was simply idle talk. Her conversations are learning experiences for her and for the people she converses with.

All three of those roles—journalist, teacher, learner—are on display in this book. The gift of this book, and I hope you enjoy it as much as I did, is that it is not just another title about how to do project-based learning. Nor is it only about how successful, cutting-edge people learn outside of school. What Suzie does is weave together both of those narratives so the reader experiences a rich picture of not only how we can use technology and project-based learning to truly transform our schools but why we should as well.

The magic of this book is Suzie's ability to braid stories of innovation from education, business, and social entrepreneurship to make her point. You will meet educators from a small Central Virginia elementary school, social entrepreneurs from New York and California, innovators as well-known as Dean Kamen and Clayton Christiansen, and even a nifty little high school in Philadelphia—and that's all in the first fifty pages. Each of those stories and the many more you will encounter create a frame, a sense of urgency, and a pathway for change.

So Suzie has written a book that is near and dear to my heart. She has taken the pedagogy most valued to me—an inquiry-driven, project-based, collaborative lens on learning—and she has shown us that when those ideas are deeply connected to the powerful tools teachers and students have at their disposal, schools can be amazing places of transformation. More than that, she has wed the work of schools to the work of prominent innovators, proving that these worlds are not far apart at all. All the while, she has raised the voices of the teachers and students in the book to the level of Steve Jobs, Sir Ken Robinson, and Jane McGonigal at a time when the practitioner voice is often being lost in the back-and-forth debate of education reform.

In the end, *Bringing Innovation to School* is not just a call to action, nor is it simply a well-told story, because at her root, Suzie is a teacher. The book is filled with practical, easy-to-follow ways to change teacher and school practice. Throughout the book, there are teachable moments, places where Suzie urges us to "Borrow This Idea," and because many of us in the trenches often don't know where to start, the entire final section of the book is a practical pathway to change, no matter where you are in the educational landscape.

We are lucky. Suzie has given us both a call for change and a blueprint for doing so. As an early reader of the book, I found myself both "cheer-reading" my way through the book—so happy that she told the stories we need to have told—and opening up Evernote to jot down ideas for discussion among the Science Leadership Academy community. By the time you are reading this, we will have read this book as a school community, looking for ways to hone our craft and push ourselves to be better tomorrow than we are today.

Thank you, Suzie, for being the amazing journalist, teacher, and learner that you are, and good luck to everyone reading. May your journey through this book be meaningful, and may it spur you to action!

Chris Lehmann

Philadelphia

April 2012

Introduction

In Bertie County, North Carolina, a class of high school students took part in a bold experiment during the 2010–11 school year. College-bound juniors were recruited for a new elective called Studio H, a hands-on immersion in the design and build process with an emphasis on local problem solving. Students were given a chance to put learning to use by designing and constructing physical improvements for their own community.

The unusual class appealed to students for a number of reasons. Most were going to be the first in their families to pursue higher education. Not only would Studio H allow them to earn early college credit from a nearby community college for applying core subjects like math, science, and writing to real-world projects, but they would also earn a stipend for a summer internship—an attractive bonus in a rural county where the poverty rate is high. It didn't hurt, either, that their new teachers were two hip design professionals who exuded energy and optimism. By facilitating the right kind of learning experience, these teachers hoped to unleash students' capacity to improve their community on the strength of their ideas.

I was eager to talk with course designer Emily Pilloton about what had unfolded in Bertie County. As a writer and consultant focusing on project-based learning, I'm always on the lookout for projects that succeed beyond expectations. Many of the quotes and observations you'll read in this book come from my classroom visits and conversations with educators. Breakthrough projects, such as Studio H, give students opportunities to take learning to new heights. Students master core academic content in the process, but that's not all. Some projects seem to flip a switch, activating students' creativity and problem-solving potential. When that happens, students discover what it means to be an innovator.

If such projects could become the norm instead of the exception, we would be well on our way to solving one of the hardest questions facing education today: how are we going to prepare a new generation of innovators? It's an urgent need, as U.S. President Barack Obama reminded us during his 2011 State of the Union address with his call to "out-innovate, out-educate, and out-build the rest of the world. That's how we'll win the future." He reinforced that message a year later, saying in his 2012 State of the Union speech, "Innovation is what America has always been about." What his remarks don't reveal, however, is how we might accomplish the ambitious goal of encouraging innovation to spread. Teaching innovative thinking remains a key challenge facing educators who are serious about preparing students for the near future.

In virtually every discussion of 21st century learning—whether it's the Framework for 21st Century Learning, the National Educational Technology Standards for Students (NETS-S), or the Common Core State Standards—innovation and its close cousin, creativity, make the list of skills that students must develop for future success. The call for innovation is coming from many quarters. Corporate leaders say they need a pipeline of good thinkers to imagine tomorrow's products. Politicians are banking on fresh ideas to drive economic growth and jump-start job creation. Citizens eager to improve the world—or just fix their corner of it—are hungry for better solutions to address persistent social and environmental problems.

Yet as teachers and students discovered in Bertie County, and as others are finding out in classrooms across the United States, there's a gap between saying we must encourage innovation and teaching students how to actually generate and execute original ideas.

When I caught up with Pilloton, Bertie County had just celebrated her students' efforts with a ribbon-cutting ceremony. For their culminating project, students designed and built a 2,000-square-foot, wood-framed pavilion for a farmers' market on land donated by the city. It gives the community a beautiful new gathering place, but that's not all. By providing a local venue for fresh produce, the market is likely to improve eating habits in a population facing rising obesity rates and related health issues. After students completed the structure, they handed over the market for the community to run. The mayor showed his gratitude by presenting students with the key to the city.

Studio H turned out to be a success by any number of measures. Nonetheless, Pilloton was quick to acknowledge that she had been overly ambitious from the start. When the first crop of students stepped into the studio the previous fall, she and her teaching partner, Matthew Miller, were in for a surprise. They envisioned Studio H as a hands-on learning experience in which students would become familiar with the same strategies that professional designers use to solve authentic problems. By helping students design and build real things,

Pilloton expected them to also build critical-thinking skills that they could transfer to solve a wide range of issues in the future. She planned to start with the basics but didn't fully appreciate what that meant. "Many of these students had never had an art class, or at least not since about fifth grade," she says. Some had never held a hammer. Many struggled to read a ruler.

Those skills, at least, seemed fairly straightforward to teach. "The biggest surprise was that students didn't have ideas coming out of their ears," Pilloton tells me, reflecting on the exhausting but exhilarating pilot year of Studio H. In her professional life, she's accustomed to the hothouse environment of the design studio. It's a place where creative types, well versed in a process for coming up with solutions, "spew ideas, and all you have to do is weed through them." But in the high school setting, she found herself with a roomful of learners who lacked confidence to think boldly. "I don't blame them," she quickly adds. "Their academic environment has not rewarded them for having crazy ideas. A big hurdle was getting them comfortable enough to raise their hand and propose something. I had no idea," she adds, "that this was going to be such a big deal."

Teaching students how to innovate is a big deal indeed. Across grade levels and subject areas, in all kinds of socioeconomic settings, I've heard teachers describe similar challenges when they shift to more active, student-driven, collaborative projects. Students used to coming up with the correct answer for a test can be confused by open-ended questions that have multiple right solutions. Students who have only been graded individually in the past may balk at a grade that reflects teamwork. A veteran elementary teacher told me how, each fall, he has to coach another class to break the habit of "holding up your hand and waiting for the teacher to tell you what to do next." Another teacher, keen to introduce her high school English class to inquiry projects, found that many students were baffled when invited to investigate questions they cared about. It turns out they had plenty of passions, but they had never thought of school as the place to pursue them.

If we're serious about preparing students to be innovators, we have some hard work ahead. Getting students ready to tackle tomorrow's challenges means helping them develop a new set of skills and fresh ways of thinking that they won't acquire through textbook-driven instruction. They need opportunities to practice these new skills on right-sized projects, with supports in place to scaffold learning. They need to persist and learn from setbacks. That's how they'll develop the confidence to tackle difficult problems. If they happen to discover their passions in the process, even better. Innovation doesn't happen without deep commitment.

I bring an unusual perspective to the topic of innovation. In the world of education, I coach and showcase the work of innovative teachers who are applying their own creativity to the design of real-world projects. I also see what students can accomplish when they have opportunities to take projects all the way from inspiration to action, and I have helped develop curricula that put students (and adults) in the role of active problem solver.

Wearing another set of lenses, I write about breakthrough ideas in the field of social change. This involves interviewing global innovators and social entrepreneurs working on issues ranging from maternal health to clean energy to improving literacy in the developing world.

Although these may seem like separate worlds, there's considerable overlap. Whether it's in a school engaged in project-based learning or in an organization tackling global poverty, success depends on knowing how to frame problems, generate ideas, test solutions, and learn from what works as well as what doesn't. Results require individual effort along with effective teamwork and often involve equal measures of passion and persistence.

Watching adult problem solvers at work, I can't help but think that this is what many of today's students might grow up to do—if they have opportunities to hone critical 21st century skills. If we can figure out how to bring innovation to school, we can offer students the training ground they need to practice authentic problem solving, conduct research, engage in genuine collaboration, and build the other skills that can lead to breakthrough ideas. Just as important, such projects will give students opportunities to investigate questions that they care about. Any teacher who has succeeded with project-based learning knows that personal engagement is what keeps students motivated during challenging projects. If a learning experience also helps them discover their passion, it can last for a lifetime.

In *How to Change the World: Social Entrepreneurs and the Power of New Ideas*, David Bornstein (2004) observes that most social entrepreneurs can recall an early-life experience when they had a chance to take a risk, explore a wild idea, or take the lead on a real-world solution close to home. It might have been finding their voice by writing for a school newspaper or learning about leadership by taking part in a community service project. One way or another, they got activated. They developed a sense of agency. Their stories remind us of the importance of nurturing innovators from a young age.

For instance, you'll hear more in a later chapter about a young innovator named Apurv Mishra who grew up in Orissa, India. He went from winning the Intel International Science and Engineering Fair as a high school student to becoming the youngest TED fellow at age nineteen to launching a global platform that tracks innovation worldwide as a young adult. Mishra has discovered that he and his fellow innovators have a "shared passion to change the world, irrespective of domains and interests" (TED blog, 2011). He also understands that they can't do this important work alone. Great ideas may start with a spark of individual inspiration, but it takes effective teamwork to put them into action.

In researching this book, I searched for schools that are setting the stage for young innovators to discover their potential as problem solvers. I found examples worth exploring at public and private schools, at comprehensive schools and charter academies, and in urban areas like Detroit and rural communities like Bertie County. As long as they were interested in teaching innovation, I was eager to hear what they were doing to encourage it.

At the same time, I kept an eye out for lessons worth borrowing from innovators who are working on some of today's biggest challenges. Their stories are inspiring as well as instructive. They deserve a place in today's classrooms alongside such American icons of innovation as the Wright brothers, Thomas Edison, George Washington Carver, Henry Ford, Grace Hopper, and more recently, Steve Jobs.

Today's innovators are as likely to be working in Africa, India, or China as in Silicon Valley. Their examples help us understand the underlying processes for developing creative solutions and bringing them to scale. Unless we hear the backstory of how these inspired ideas have come about, however, innovation can seem like a magic elixir. By examining their stories for innovation strategies, we can remove the mystery without diluting the potency of innovation.

As you'll discover in the following chapters, there's more than one way to bring innovation to school. You'll hear about projects involving design thinking, engineering, tinkering, and the creative arts. You'll hear about examples across subject areas and grade levels, such as middle schoolers learning about social studies by taking part in microlending and high school students improving their writing and communication skills through digital gaming.

What unites these examples is the underlying belief that innovation is both powerful and teachable. In the business world, innovation is what drives product development. In the social sector, it's how good thinkers are tackling seemingly intractable problems like poverty and climate change. And in the classroom, a more deliberate focus on encouraging innovation across the curriculum is how teachers will build students' 21st century skills as problem solvers, critical thinkers, capable communicators, and collaborators.

It's not enough for students to have ideas "coming out of their ears," as Pilloton put it. They also need to know what to do next to put a worthy idea into action. Teaching students how to innovate is about both thinking and doing. In that spirit, this book is organized in three parts to help you think and do.

Part I sets the stage by introducing a common language for talking about innovation and the qualities of innovators and for understanding why innovation is so essential for today's students. Chapter 1, "Coming to Terms With Innovation," discusses ways to encourage innovation in schools and provides several examples that show how to unleash creative thinking and better define *innovation*. Chapter 2, "Seeing Educators as Innovators," asks you to consider your innovation profile—how can you become an innovation role model for your students? Chapter 3, "Growing a New Global Skill Set," introduces the possible global impact innovation can have when students ask authentic questions, think big, build empathy, and work with passion.

Part II goes inside the new idea factory for a look at schools that are making innovation a priority. Within each chapter, a Strategy Spotlight highlights a way of thinking used by innovators in diverse contexts, with ready applications to teaching and learning. Chapter 4, "Seeding Innovation," shows how Albemarle County Public Schools challenged everyone in the district to innovate in a bottom-up manner—growing ideas—to produce an environment that encourages creative problem solving. Chapter 5, "Integrating Design Thinking Throughout the Curriculum," introduces the Henry Ford Learning Institute network, where students are immersed in the process of design thinking in a way that connects design challenges to academic standards. Chapter 6, "Making Room for Thinkers," details how to change the physical space and the schedules in order to better accommodate innovation. Chapter 7, "Taking Advantage of Technology," shows how emerging technology—specifically the tabletop digital fabricator, a kind of 3-D printer—can help students learn innovation strategies and processes as early as the elementary grades. Chapter 8, "Gaming for Real Learning," details how teachers can use student interest in gaming to develop projects with real-world implications.

Part III suggests action steps to move forward with an innovation agenda. Chapter 9, "Spreading Good Ideas," shares the stories of educators who have used their professional networks to extend the impact of effective strategies. Chapter 10, "Taking Action," shares first steps to taking action now, including finding your edge, developing common processes, removing barriers, finding allies, practicing innovative teaching, encouraging innovation in informal learning, and showcasing results.

The appendices include additional resources, a sample innovation rubric, and a discussion guide.

Throughout the book, watch for the following special features to help you apply ideas about innovation to your own school context:

- **Action Step**—This prompt challenges you to take an action designed to advance your innovation agenda.

- **Borrow This Idea**—Watch for this prompt for ready-to-try suggestions or projects for the classroom.

- **How to Get Started**—This prompt suggests first steps or considerations to help you implement a promising idea in your learning community.

Part I

Setting the Stage

Starting with the end in mind is a well-regarded approach for designing learning experiences. What's the end goal for bringing innovation to school? It helps to begin with a common language for talking about this big idea. It's also worth considering the qualities of innovators so that educators can encourage these habits of mind in their students—and in themselves. Finally, we need to consider the new skills that will be required to help us reach the goal of a more innovative society. Part I sets the stage for this transformation by building your background knowledge about innovation.

Chapter 1

Coming to Terms With Innovation

On a chilly weekend each January, about five hundred teachers, school leaders, students, and others come together for EduCon, an event known for sparking deep conversation about thinking and learning. Hosted by Science Leadership Academy, a public high school in Philadelphia with a national reputation for excellence, each EduCon focuses on a different theme. In 2011, it was innovation. At the Friday-night kickoff event at the Franklin Museum, a panel of esteemed thinkers demonstrated the difficulty of coming to terms with this word that we hear with such great frequency.

Frederic Bertley, vice president of science and innovation at the Franklin Institute, launched the discussion by sharing a collection of quotes about innovation:

- Steve Jobs, Apple cofounder—"Innovation distinguishes between a leader and a follower."

- Margaret Wheatley, expert on leadership—"Innovation is collaboration."

- President Barack Obama—"Innovation is how we make our living."

- Ben Franklin, legendary innovator—"When you're finished changing, you're finished."

Of course, these are just a handful of the definitions that get tossed around. Some days it feels as if we're at risk of innovation overload, with marketers of everything from breakfast cereal to hair products claiming to be innovators. But definitions matter, especially when you're trying to set the stage for innovation. This chapter will help you clarify your understanding of innovation and understand why it's considered such an urgent goal for today's students.

The Evolution of Innovation

John Kao, a self-described innovation activist (as well as an angel investor, jazz pianist, psychiatrist, and former Harvard Business School professor), is an excellent guide to understanding this territory. He reminds us that innovation is not static. It's an evolving concept. In *Innovation Nation*, Kao (2007) outlines four historical stages of innovation:

1.0—We begin with the tradition of individual inventors following their curiosity and practicing what Kao calls the "artisanal model of innovation." Think Ben Franklin and his kite or the Wright brothers tinkering with their flying machine.

2.0—The industrial era of innovation brings us thinkers like Thomas Edison and Henry Ford, who set up idea factories and centralized research labs to improve industry.

3.0—Deinstitutionalized innovation opens the era of the innovator-entrepreneur financed by venture capital. Entrepreneurial communities, like Silicon Valley, expand through open networks enabled by Internet and digital collaboration.

4.0—Global diffusion of innovation brings us to today. New ideas are originating anywhere and everywhere. Innovation is flattened.

Across these eras, Kao defines innovation as "the ability of individuals, companies, and entire nations to continuously create their desired future . . . It is about new ways of doing and seeing things as much as it is about the breakthrough idea" (2007, p. 19).

Steve Johnson (2010), in *Where Good Ideas Come From*, also endorses a definition that is deliberately expansive. By *innovation*, he simply means good ideas. Looking broadly helps him see the common processes and patterns that give rise to innovation in all sorts of contexts. "The poet and the engineer (and the coral reef) may seem a million miles apart in their particular forms of expertise, but when they bring good ideas into the world, similar patterns of development and collaboration shape the process" (Johnson, 2010, p. 22).

Innovation expert Clayton Christensen adds more complexity to the definition by introducing the concept of disruptive innovation. Disruption often comes from new, lower-cost products like personal computers or mobile phones, which challenge and eventually take over more established products. Apple's earliest personal computer, for instance, didn't begin to compare in computing power with the high-priced minicomputers or mainframe computers then on the market. "All it had to do was make a product that was better than the customers' other alternative, which was no computer at all," Christensen explains in *Disrupting Class* (Christensen, Horn, & Johnson, 2011, p. 73). Eventually, such disruptions move "up market," transforming the whole space. The once-disruptive technology becomes the new normal.

Like technologists, social innovators also look for opportunities to disrupt old patterns. They tackle social and environmental challenges with strategies more often found in the business world than in the non-profit sector. But their goal is social good rather than bottom-line benefits. Instead of operating traditional charities such as soup kitchens to feed the hungry, social entrepreneurs might launch restaurants that double as job-training sites for the chronically unemployed. Greyston Bakery in Yonkers, New York, captures this way of thinking with its tagline: "We don't hire people to bake brownies. We bake brownies to hire people." Social entrepreneurs are also clever at tapping new funding sources to make good ideas sustainable. TOMS Shoes, for instance, gives away a pair of shoes to a child in need for every pair purchased. For children growing up in the developing world, shoes promote better health by providing a barrier against soil-transmitted diseases and infections. Although some social innovators are well-known for their breakthrough ideas—such as Nobel Laureate Muhammad Yunus, credited with developing the global concept of microlending—many are quietly hard at work on important issues in their communities. In their own backyards, students can find accessible role models who are tackling difficult problems, fine-tuning solutions, and spreading good ideas. These problem solvers help students understand that there's a need for innovators across society.

Consider a social innovator like Gary Maxworthy. After a successful career in the commercial food industry, he volunteered to work with a local food bank. He was amazed by what he learned from the experience. In California alone, where he lives, some five million people can't afford the food they need. The problem isn't food scarcity. California produces more than half the nation's fruits, nuts, and vegetables. Maxworthy discovered that tons of produce are left to rot each year because there's no system for salvaging less-than-perfect fruits and vegetables. Meanwhile, food banks never have enough fresh produce to nourish the hungry.

Bringing a fresh perspective to these issues, Maxworthy reframed the problem of feeding the hungry. He helped design a new, statewide distribution system called Farm to Family that solves two problems at once: growers get a reliable way to dispose of the slightly blemished produce that they would otherwise pay to send to the dump, and food banks get a centrally managed supply of nourishing, fresh food. More than one hundred million pounds of produce annually are distributed to needy families through this award-winning program. His approach illustrates a strategy common to innovators: they recognize opportunities that others overlook.

Students are also capable of this kind of thinking. Two fourth graders at an elementary school in Southern California recently made headlines for convincing their school to start a lunch recycling program. The girls were troubled by the amount of untouched food that went into the trash each day. Determined to do something about it, they started by gathering data to fully understand the issue (developing their research skills). They graphed the results, showing the value of five hundred discarded items a week (putting math skills to authentic use). Then they advocated to change the system with a letter-writing campaign (applying language arts skills) that eventually attracted the interest of the mayor. As a result of their proposal, students' unopened leftovers are now deposited on a common table in the school cafeteria and collected by a social service agency that feeds hungry families.

Students who have acquired an innovator's mindset learn that they can apply problem-solving strategies in almost any context. The application part is essential. By implementing their food recycling solution, students in the previous example discovered that they have the ability to put good ideas into action now. They don't have to wait to be adults to start making a difference.

It shouldn't be surprising that the very meaning of innovation continues to evolve. That makes sense to Chris Lehmann, founding principal of Science Leadership Academy and host of EduCon. He says, "Innovation on some level is evolution not revolution. It's the idea of taking something and making it better. It's about deepening and enriching."

Innovation Unleashed

In 2010, the U.S. Department of Education awarded $650 million in competitive grants through its Investing in Innovation Fund, known as i3. The idea was to encourage innovation in public education and also attract foundation dollars to stretch federal funding and bring worthy ideas to a larger scale.

A year later, however, a study by Bellwether Education Partners questioned whether the funds had uncovered any significant breakthroughs. The largest grants, $50 million apiece, went to already well-known programs such as Teach for America and KIPP Academy. These programs had demonstrated effectiveness and were considered ready to expand. Another thirty organizations received no more than $5 million each for proposals that were considered promising. But even these ideas were expected to show evidence of effectiveness. That meant winning ideas had to be well into the phase of implementation and evaluation—hence, past the stage where there's room to play with solutions. One applicant remarked, "Neither the iPhone or iPad teams at Apple would have been able to meet this standard to get the funds to initiate these projects" (Smith & Petersen, 2011, p. 24).

Although i3 was intended to attract new funding to promising approaches, some philanthropists reported being disappointed in the caliber of ideas to choose from. One funder said, "Out of the development grants, I would be amazed if these grantees really develop into game-changers" (Smith & Petersen, 2011, p. 45).

That shouldn't be surprising, given that the process didn't encourage risk-taking or a willingness to learn from failure—two hallmarks of innovators that we'll hear more about in the next chapter.

Compare this relative scarcity of innovation to the range of ideas that get unleashed when the definition is less restrictive. Let's look at three examples that show how to cast a wider net for creative thinking: No Right Brain Left Behind, Maker Faire, and Kickstarter.

No Right Brain Left Behind

No Right Brain Left Behind was a recent innovation-in-education competition for advertising agencies, design consultancies, and others whose bread and butter is creativity. Instead of hand-wringing about the creativity crisis in American education, they challenged each other to come up with solutions during a five-day event in 2011, timed to coincide with Social Media Week. Judges included well-known creativity expert Sir Ken Robinson.

Judging criteria offered a detailed but still open-ended definition. Points would be awarded for ideas that didn't already exist in the marketplace, would be easy for educators to adopt and feasible given currently available technologies, offered potential to overcome current constraints in the education system, fostered creativity in children, and reignited students' passion for learning. And then there was this final caveat: It is not about creating more artists. We're looking for ideas that will teach kids to use creativity to solve tomorrow's problems. They'll need both sides of their brains to successfully face the challenges of the 21st century.

Within five days, three hundred wildly divergent entries poured in. The Stand-Up Desk, proposed by The Bucket Brigade, grows out of the idea that changing the learning environment can lead to more creativity. The desk features include a whiteboard top that flips up to become an easel, so that students can work on problems, share ideas, or lead discussions. Another proposal, Kings and Queens of Creativity, by Hyper Island Stockholm, turns problem solving into a game. Here's the idea: schools join by submitting a real challenge they are facing. Then, fellow participants engage by offering up creative solutions to other schools' problems, learning along the way how to evaluate solutions, build on each other's ideas, and be persuasive. The winning entry, Right-Brain Revolution, submitted by Proximity Chicago/ Energy BBDO, proposes a reality show about education. Right-Brain Revolution would showcase teacher and student creativity across the country, generating positive buzz about education and promoting a national exchange of worthy ideas—of which, it's implied, there's no shortage.

Maker Faire

In a different context, Maker Faire events offer a thriving example of grassroots innovation, with an educational flavor. Since the first Maker Faire in San Mateo, California, in 2006, the idea has spawned a global network of events that celebrate the innovation of the DIY (do-it-yourself) or Maker movement. Part of the appeal is the playful spirit of this community. Michelle Hlubinka (2011), education director for Maker Faire, describes the typical event as a meet-up of "over 600 Makers (or people who 'make things') exhibiting their projects in arts, craft, engineering, food, health, music, science, and technology. Rockets to robots, felting to beekeeping, pedal-power to mobile muffin cars—you never know what you'll see at Maker Faire."

Whether it takes place in California, Detroit, or Africa, Maker Faire offers a setting where fresh ideas are welcome. Indeed, these fairs not only coax zany projects out of the woodwork but create community and connections among participants, as well as a chance to learn together. A guide to organizing your own Maker Faire describes the community that comes together:

> Maker Faire provides a venue for Makers to show examples of their work and interact with others about it. Many Makers tell us that they have no other place to show what they do. It is often out of the spotlight of traditional art or science or craft events. DIY often is invisible in our communities, taking place in shops, garages and kitchen tables. So the goal of the event is to make visible the projects and ideas that we don't encounter every day. Maker Faire, like any fair, might include traditional forms of making but it is primarily designed to be forward-looking, exploring new forms and new technologies. (Maker Faire, 2011)

What's more, Maker Faire is about cooperation and participation rather than competition. Exhibitors often come away from events with ideas for product improvements, thanks to fairgoers and fellow exhibitors who offer up insights and pitch in to troubleshoot technical glitches. "We get to learn how things work, and why. We get to try new things and understand that we can expand our own capabilities. We consider the process of making as important as the perfect, finished product. Sharing the process with others creates new opportunities for learning" (Maker Faire, 2011). Thanks to efforts by Hlubinka and others, this initiative—and its expansive definition of innovation—is spreading into educational settings with Maker Clubs designed to boost students' creativity.

Kickstarter

Kickstarter offers a third example of how to unlock creativity. This crowd-funding platform is itself an innovation. It allows people with ideas to raise money online for creative projects, bypassing the typical funding barriers between inspiration and implementation. Projects vary widely: documentary films on socially significant topics like child slavery, architectural initiatives that promise to revive neighborhoods, and oddball inventions like an edible cup. But not just any old idea qualifies. Proposals have to make it through an approval process that screens out charitable giving. Nor does Kickstarter accept what it calls "fund my life" requests (such as pay my tuition or send me on a vacation) or ideas that generally lack a creative purpose. And qualifying ideas have to be genuine projects, not ongoing initiatives, with clearly defined goals and expectations.

On the flip side, Kickstarter gives ordinary folks a chance to back innovative ideas, kicking in a few dollars to help fund the kind of project that would typically depend on securing a grant or attracting an angel. Supporters get no creative ownership. Instead, their small pledges (average pledge size is $25) might bring them rewards like an arty tee-shirt or invitation to a film premiere. Three years after Kickstarter's launch in 2009, more than twenty-two thousand ideas had been successfully funded, with pledge totals topping $200 million, making it the world's largest funding platform for creative projects.

Those who manage to get funded on Kickstarter are good at telling their stories with social media. Like innovators from other fields, they know how to network. They generate buzz via YouTube, Facebook, and Twitter. They attract donors not only with their creative thinking but with their passion to act on their ideas. Kickstarter encourages this sense of urgency. Each project pitch must include a specific funding goal, a countdown clock, and an all-or-nothing proposition: make or exceed your goal in time, and it's all yours (minus a small percentage to Kickstarter). Fall short, and no money changes hands.

When it comes to encouraging innovation, we can either hold back the flood of ideas by imposing too many restrictions, or we can encourage ideas to grow by allowing for small risks, collaboration, and even playfulness. A definition that incorporates these conditions is a good starting place for introducing innovation to the classroom.

The Urgency to Innovate

American inventor Dean Kamen, creator of the insulin pump and the Segway scooter, considers genuine innovation to be both difficult and rare. Inventions are more commonplace. Kamen estimates that the number of inventions registered at the U.S. Patent Office has soared by four million during his adulthood. Yet true innovation, he argues, "changes the way people live or think or work or understand the world they live in" (Hurd, 2010). Such breakthroughs don't come along very often.

If innovators are indeed a rare breed, then why should educators invest precious classroom time and acquire new instructional strategies to nurture this capacity in students?

So far, the loudest voices about the need to innovate in education have been coming from outside the world of teaching and learning. The Partnership for 21st Century Skills, an organization founded by technology and communications industry leaders, emphasizes innovation as an essential component of its Framework for 21st Century Learning. Being able to work in new ways on new problems is seen as a key career skill. Many of today's students will likely enter careers not yet imagined and make use of technologies not yet invented. As economist Richard Florida (2002) explains, "The ability to come up with new ideas and better ways of doing things is ultimately what raises productivity and thus living standards" (p. xiii).

Anticipated shortages in the fields known as STEM—science, technology, engineering, and math—add more urgency. President Obama and a chorus of corporate CEOs call for STEM education to build a pipeline for future innovation, whether that means developing green energy, devising medical breakthroughs, or coming up with the next wave of consumer technologies.

The need for innovators crosses sectors as well as geographies. Consider the names that appeared on *Fast Company*'s list of most creative leaders for 2011. Physician Paul Farmer has pioneered effective new ways of delivering health care to the poor in Haiti, Rwanda, and other developing countries. David Kobia is director of technology development for Ushahidi. This open-source network, which grew out of a post-election crisis in Kenya, develops software for information-gathering, data visualization, and mapping. Rounding out *Fast Company*'s list were executives from Google, Apple, and familiar names from the worlds of media and entertainment.

Today's students are growing up at a time when new ideas are emerging from all corners of the globe. In the United States, national pride can sometimes make innovation seem like an American invention. U.S. citizens rightly celebrate the can-do spirit that lifted the Wright brothers into history and the spark of inspiration that led Thomas Edison to build his idea factory. But the next wave of breakthrough ideas may be coming from halfway around the world instead of from domestic hot spots like Silicon Valley. To be part of this innovation economy, students have to be able to connect across cultures.

With information flattened and new forms of collaboration possible due to technology, distressed economic conditions are no longer a barrier to innovation. Indeed, constraints can be a springboard for new ways of thinking and problem solving.

In India, where resources are insufficient to reach a billion people, innovation happens despite scarcity. Indians calls this *jugaad*, or frugal innovation. This mindset has given rise to products like the Tata Nano, the world's cheapest car, and a cloud-based tablet computer called the Aakash that retails for less than fifty dollars. In Africa, no-frills mobile phones are providing new platforms for banking and retail. Some frugal ideas are starting to make their way from less-developed countries to wealthier regions. In a connected world, no corner of the globe owns innovation.

Future.ly is an online platform that aims to map innovation across the world. It's the latest brainchild of Apurv Mishra, the young innovator from India we met in the introduction who is convinced that countries like China and India could become the next hub of innovation. Future.ly aims to track that process and make it visible.

There's good reason to pay attention to Mishra. He first gained global attention as a high school student, when he won top prize in the Intel International Science and Engineering Fair. His winning invention, called the Glabenator, uses small muscle movements in the forehead to control a computer, enabling a person who is paralyzed (or temporarily immobilized, such as a pilot under extreme G forces) to communicate with others. He was inspired to develop the device after watching his grandfather struggle to talk after suffering a stroke.

Mishra's inventiveness is impressive, but he also has extreme skills when it comes to networking. After meeting hundreds of similarly inspiring teens at the international science fair, he realized that worthy ideas from young innovators—especially those in the developing world—need support if they're ever going to be implemented. So he launched an open platform called the Innovator Factor Foundation to connect young thinkers with the critique and support they need to put ideas into action.

Future.ly is taking that kind of thinking to another level with the application of data mining, visualization tools, and a determination to "crack the innovation genome." By recognizing the innovative work underway in all parts of the world, Mishra hopes to accelerate tomorrow's breakthroughs. "Innovation is not just suddenly there; it builds up, sometimes at unexpected speeds. Tomorrow's innovation is a result of the culmination of the relentless and pioneering effort of today's innovators. These pioneers, who foresee and work toward a vision, drive our future," he explained in an interview on the TED blog (2011).

The case for encouraging more innovation is not just economic. Addressing the myriad global problems in front of us will require thinkers who can come at problems from diverse perspectives. Today's youth face escalating costs for housing, health care, and education and a world population of seven billion putting unprecedented pressures on already-scarce resources. Solving these looming social and environmental issues around the world will demand breakthrough ideas and new capacities to collaborate across cultures.

The *Horizon Report*, an annual project of the New Media Consortium's Emerging Technology Initiative, looks across disciplines to predict which trends are poised to affect teaching, learning, and creative inquiry. The 2010 report for K–12 concludes,

> The perceived value of innovation and creativity is increasing. Innovation is valued at the highest levels of business and must be embraced in schools if students are to succeed beyond their formal education. The ways we design learning experiences must reflect the growing importance of innovation and creativity as professional skills. Innovation and creativity must not be linked only to arts subjects, either; these skills are equally important in scientific inquiry, entrepreneurship, and other areas as well. (Johnson, Smith, Levine, & Haywood, 2010, p. 4)

Creativity Shortfall

Creativity and innovation are so closely related that the terms often are used interchangeably. The Framework for 21st Century Skills, for example, combines them into a singular goal. The distinctions are subtle but worth considering. In broad strokes, creativity is about generating original ideas. We may recognize it most easily in the arts, where creativity is both a means of personal expression and a reflection of culture. But creativity extends well beyond the arts; it's a defining quality of being human. In comparison, innovation feels more practical. It's also about fresh thinking, but the focus is on moving good ideas forward so that positive change occurs. One innovation often sets the stage for more good things to happen, reshaping a system to a new normal. In breakthrough projects, we can find both the initial spark of creativity and the application of innovation processes.

Success in a wide range of careers now requires the kind of creative thinking previously reserved for the arts. A recent IBM poll of fifteen hundred CEOs from sixty nations identified creativity as the top leadership competency of the future (Carr, 2010).

Yet even as the demand for more inventive thinkers mushrooms, there are worrisome signs that U.S. youth are losing their creative edge. Kyung Hee Kim, an education psychologist at the College of William and Mary, has become a leading voice about declining creativity in American children. She examined three hundred thousand scores on the Torrance Test of Creative Thinking and found that creativity scores started dropping in the 1990s. The decline is most serious for American youth in grades K–6.

Steady cuts in arts education don't help address this decline. Yet creativity involves more than artistic expression. The Torrance Test measures creative potential in art, literature, science, mathematics, leadership, and interpersonal relationships. The test also measures so-called creative strengths: being energetic, talkative, unconventional, humorous, and lively or passionate. Students with creative strengths are able to see things from different angles and connect seemingly irrelevant things. Rather than encouraging these behaviors, however, many traditional classrooms would label them as disruptive to learning.

Yong Zhao, born and raised in China and now an education professor at the University of Oregon, makes a similar case about the precarious state of American creativity. In *Catching Up or Leading the Way*, he writes, "Creativity, interpreted as both ability and passion to make new things and adapt to new situations, is essential . . . a must for living in the new age" (2009, p. 151). Yet he worries that U.S. schools, once the world leader at producing innovative thinkers, are turning their backs on this strength in their quest for higher standardized test scores. Zhao continues developing this argument on his blog:

> The most serious and well-documented costs [of high-stakes tests] are the loss of opportunities for students to have access to a broad range of educational experiences as well as the opportunity to develop the ability and skills that truly matter in the 21st century, such as creativity and global competence . . . America may succeed in raising test scores but it will likely end up as a nation of great test takers in an intellectually barren land. (2011)

Zhao warns us that this has happened before. For generations, China used an imperial testing system called *keju* to cull candidates for elite government positions. "It has been blamed as a cause of China's failure to develop modern science, technology, and enterprises as well as China's repeated failures in wars with foreign powers because good test takers are just that: good at taking tests and nothing else," Zhao (2011) writes. Today, while the United States narrows the curriculum and focuses on improving test scores, China is going full tilt on educational reforms that will build the soft skills needed to drive an innovation-based economy (Zhao, 2011).

A few pioneering states are responding to these concerns by developing indexes that will track the opportunities schools provide to encourage creative thinking. That's a trend worth watching; such efforts could give teachers and school leaders more incentives to focus on innovation and creative problem solving within the curriculum.

Student Interest as a Catalyst for Innovation

So far, student voices have not been heard much in discussions about innovation in education. That may be changing. Students are starting to speak with their actions. Innovating to solve global challenges is an idea that clearly appeals to many of today's youth.

For three days in 2011, global leaders from telecommunications and technology industries gathered in Geneva, Switzerland, for the annual International Telecommunications Union (ITU) World Conference, a project of the United Nations. Meanwhile, some ten thousand students from five continents took part virtually through the ITU Telecom World Meta Conference.

While the adults were busy with high-level discussions about the global impact of new technologies and faster broadband, students were prototyping solutions to real-world problems. They used the design thinking process—a framework for problem solving that involves repeat cycles of researching, brainstorming, prototyping, and testing solutions—to tackle issues such as poverty alleviation, gender inequality, and access to health care and education. Their suggested solutions—which had to meet criteria of being tangible, pragmatic, and "make-able"—included wheelchairs with built-in cell phones, a seed exchange to help villagers grow their way out of hunger, and smartphone apps to prevent food spoilage. Ewan McIntosh, a veteran educator who facilitated the youth event through his consulting organization, NoTosh, reflected afterward that the impact on learning "has been profound. It's the one project that has made students feel that their voice and ideas are worth something, that their learning has been 'for real.'"

Youthful energy for problem solving is similarly evident at Imagine Cup, an international event sponsored by Microsoft. Student teams design digital games and software that address the United Nations Millennium Development Goals. Participation has skyrocketed since the contest was refocused a few years ago to connect to these global challenges.

Focusing students' digital creativity on improving literacy, reducing poverty, or curing malaria offers the world "a chance for an epic win," according to celebrated game designer Jane McGonigal. "This age group—the Millennials—seems to put a higher value on being of service to a larger cause than previous generations," she told me at the U.S. finals of Imagine Cup in 2011. "Combine that with their interest in technology and love of gaming, and it seems like a powerful one-two punch that will escalate the quality of serious projects."

Two young competitors at Imagine Cup were from Lick-Wilmerding High School in San Francisco. Xander Masotto and Julius Lee developed a strategy game called Strain that challenges players to defend the world against a global pandemic. Their carefully researched idea offers a positive alternative to commercial games that unleash pandemics on virtual worlds. As Masotto explains, "We thought, what if the goal was to save people instead of killing them?" It's the kind of project that requires critical thinking and applications of biology, geography, and computer science content, along with collaboration and communications skills. Yet it wasn't assigned for a class. These motivated students found time to pursue the project outside the regular school day, exhibiting the passion that defines innovators at any age.

By leveraging their passions during the school day, we can give students more opportunities to connect what they are studying with the real-world issues they care about. That's how students will define innovation on their own terms, as something that will enable them to shape their future. In the long run, engaging student passions may be our best strategy for bringing innovation to school.

Action Step

Define what *learning to innovate* means to you today, in the context of your school, your district, or even your specific subject area or grade level. Your definition may evolve, but having a clear starting point will focus your thinking. Knowing what you mean by innovation will help you design projects to encourage or deepen specific skills. It will help you plan authentic assessments that measure what students know and can do as innovators. (For a sample innovation rubric, see appendix B, page 141.) It will also ensure that you and your colleagues are using the same language to discuss what it means to innovate.

To frame your thinking, consider the qualities of innovators (these will be further described in chapter 2). Table 1.1 shows the dispositions and skills that students should develop as they grow into this role.

Table 1.1: Qualities of Student Innovators

A student who is . . .	Will be . . .
Action-oriented	Able to recognize problems, advocate for worthy solutions
A networker	Able to collaborate, build on others' ideas, access resources
A risk-taker	Willing to suggest or consider unconventional solutions
Forward-looking	Able to anticipate consequences and benefits, recognize potential for game-changing ideas
Able to overcome obstacles	Persistent, able to apply problem-solving strategies to overcome setbacks
Able to help good ideas grow	Able to attract others to support an idea

What else belongs in your definition of *learning to innovate*?

Expand your thinking by working the way innovators do: Invite feedback on your definition. Welcome multiple perspectives (including students' opinions). Expand on your colleagues' suggestions. As you learn more, continue refining and improving on your effort to define what it means to learn to innovate.

Borrow This Idea

What's the backstory of a breakthrough? Put students in the role of investigator, historian, or storyteller to explain how today's problem solvers arrive at their breakthrough ideas, products, or solutions. This open-ended topic invites students to bring their own passions into the project. They should choose a person or team to profile from a field that most interests them (science or medicine, environmental or social issues, popular culture, politics, technology, and so on), and investigate the context, habits of mind, work ethic, pressures, and sometimes good fortune that lead to success. (See appendix A, page 135, for resources about innovators from a variety of fields.) Uncovering the backstory of a good idea may involve doing background reading, investigating artifacts, conducting original interviews, challenging media mythology, making evaluations of impact, and so forth. Students' final products could vary widely—curated exhibits, presentations, digital stories, reenactments—as students decide how to tell the real story of success.

Chapter 2

Seeing Educators as Innovators

Michael Thornton's fourth-grade classroom sits a stone's throw from the birthplace of Meriwether Lewis in the foothills of the Blue Ridge Mountains. Not surprisingly, the school is named for the legendary explorer who risked life and limb to catalog the wonders of the American West. But although history is abundant in Albemarle County, Virginia, the future is where Thornton tries to focus his students' attention.

"I'm always telling them, *you can be the one*," says the young teacher as he folds himself into a chair designed for a ten-year-old. He grew up not far from where he now teaches and hasn't lost the energy and curiosity that sometimes made him restless as a student. Thornton's message to today's students: "*You can be the one* who makes the technology or tool that will change everything." He regularly introduces students to powerful tools like Skype, which he uses to connect his classroom with people around the world, including parents who are traveling on business. "How cool is that?" he says. "I remind them that someone had to invent this technology. I tell them to think ten years into the future. What's it going to be? Who's going to invent the next tool? They all need to be thinking this way."

His radar is always up for chances to reinforce this message. In late 2010, when Thornton heard that thirty-three miners were about to be rescued from a cave-in deep in the earth in Chile, he made sure his students were tuned in to the television coverage. Getting them to empathize with the miners and their dramatic story was part of his motivation. He also wanted to make sure his students knew about the team of scientists and engineers who had been working around the clock to make the rescue happen. As wide-eyed students watched the rescue pod make its vertical ascent, bringing the first miner toward daylight, they understood that designing this contraption had required overcoming a host of challenges and recovering from one failure after another.

Thornton first had to go through his own mental calculus before deciding that the miners' rescue was worth an investment of class time. Would this conversation connect to the fourth-grade curriculum and learning standards, or would it be an interesting distraction? On standardized tests, there was not likely to be a single question about the Chilean miners. But in his grade-level science standards, Thornton could point to several learning goals about simple and complex machines. Problem solving and global awareness are also important learning goals for 21st century students, and there were strong connections here to social studies standards. For a number of reasons, he recognized this as a topic worth pursuing.

Was it time well spent? The short answer came while students were still watching the rescue unfold. One boy said, "Maybe I'll be the one who comes up with something to save someone's life someday." Thornton was quick to chime in. "Yes! That's the concept you need to have in your minds all the time. Anything you learn, think about how it can be used in life. *You can be the one.* That's what innovation is about."

Fortunately for these students and this teacher, Albemarle County Public Schools is a district that has chosen to embrace innovation. When Superintendent Pam Moran talks about pursuing innovation, she's not giving lip service to a popular phrase. Innovative thinking is something she welcomes—indeed, encourages—from teachers like Thornton. He doesn't have to fly under the radar when he wants to test-drive a new approach. Instead, he can submit a proposal to the district to get an action research idea funded for his classroom. (In chapter 4, we'll hear more about the district's strategies for building an innovation culture across the thirteen-thousand-student district.)

The first step in teaching students to innovate is making sure that educators have opportunities to be innovators themselves. Although some teachers attempt this hard work alone, the culture of a school or district can set the stage for innovation to flourish—or flounder. The right conditions include a shared vision and common language for talking about innovation, both of which we'll explore in more detail. With those pieces in place, educators have more room to design, improve on, and share learning experiences that will stretch their students' thinking skills.

In schools across the United States, teachers across grade levels, subject areas, and diverse contexts are employing deliberate approaches to nurture a new generation of thinkers. As you'll see, their efforts don't diminish learning goals related to mastering content. Instead, they extend standards-based instruction to emphasize the 21st century skills of collaboration, critical thinking, creativity, and global awareness that can lead to innovation.

Model Innovators

Some of the instructional ideas in this book are still in the pilot stage, too new to have an extensive research base. More formal study is underway and will be important for making the case for expanding programs like design thinking and children's engineering within the standards-based, K–12 curriculum, or community-based tinkering studios for informal learning.

Yet even at this early stage, we can learn plenty from classrooms on the leading edge of teaching innovation. They offer us a Skunk Works—a research-and-development lab—where students aren't waiting to innovate. They're already hard at work on projects that have the potential to improve the world or even just fix a nearby corner of it. Students are becoming not only better thinkers, but also makers, doers, and problem solvers.

Consider just a few examples. At St. Gregory College Preparatory School in Tucson, Arizona, students can earn a special high school diploma in innovation if they can prove they have the chops by developing a mobile app, solar-powered charging station for electronic devices, or other product or approach that addresses a real need. In Redmond, Washington, youth are teaching adults how to lessen their carbon footprint, starting with a classroom-by-classroom Cool School Challenge. In North Carolina, middle-school students are global philanthropists with their own microlending club and portfolio of investments in low-income communities around the world.

These aren't random projects. Each was started deliberately, with a considered approach to providing more relevant learning opportunities. They give students the chance to learn and apply core academic concepts, providing real-world contexts for standards-based content. They incorporate authentic assessment, challenging students to demonstrate what they know or can do as a result of their learning experience.

Through these experiences, students develop and practice the skills for innovative thinking described in broad strokes in the Framework for 21st Century Skills and the National Educational Technology

Standards for Students. These documents do a good job of describing the *what* when it comes to teaching innovation. They catalog essential skills, such as knowing how to generate worthwhile ideas, learn from failure, and communicate effectively. Innovative projects take us to the next step and demonstrate *how* to make these important skills teachable by guiding students through the process of innovating.

Emily Pilloton, the designer-instructor you met in the introduction, understands the importance of *how*. She wisely recognized that her Studio H students needed preparation before tackling a large-scale project for their community. To build their background knowledge about design as well as their thinking skills, she first led them through critical discussions about architecture. As she explains, "We looked at examples [of built environments] that are considered successful and dissected them." Just as English students use critical thinking to analyze literary techniques when studying a piece of writing, Studio H students learned to critique the qualities of built projects from different perspectives, such as human scale, environmental impact, and use of materials. This exercise helped them develop their own "litmus test for what constitutes successful design," Pilloton explains, "and also gave them the mind to critique something." Once they had a vocabulary and context for talking about design, she says, "they were more willing to start proposing their own ideas. The ice floes started to move."

From there, students tackled small-scale projects intended to teach specific skills. Their first assignment: design and build a wooden board for a beanbag-toss game. "It was the perfect object to learn about simple wood construction and also graphic design," Pilloton says. "Students had to think about color theory, proportion and scale, and why graphic design is important."

Next, they moved on to designing and building chicken coops. This assignment addressed a number of important learning goals while serving an authentic purpose. Their region had recently suffered a flood that left many families homeless or lacking the basics. "Giving them chicken coops would help families that needed a sustainable food source," Pilloton explains.

Designing coops was also a right-sized introduction to architecture. The assignment started with something familiar. The county is a poultry-growing region, and many parents either raise chickens or work at a large chicken processing plant. In the design studio, students were challenged to think more critically about something familiar.

"We started by talking about, here's what we know of chickens. Here's another way to look," Pilloton says. She and her teaching colleague participated in these conversations, modeling divergent thinking. "Matt and I were not afraid to pitch the wackiest things. We pushed them to go beyond what a chicken coop looked like in their head. We wanted them to realize that some crazy ideas are actually wonderful."

Getting those ideas onto paper gave students practice with sketch modeling and, later, 3-D prototyping by building cardboard models. Gradually, through critical feedback and multiple revisions, their ideas took shape. Pilloton says, "They came up with some of the weirdest-looking chicken coops you've ever seen." But weird looks weren't enough. Before getting the go-ahead to build their coops, students had to make a case for the functional benefits of their designs.

After these introductory projects, students were ready to tackle the farmers' market design, which required using their new toolkit of problem-solving strategies to handle a fresh set of challenges. (In chapter 5, we'll hear more from schools that are introducing design thinking into the K–12 curriculum.)

Like Pilloton, the teachers and school leaders you'll meet in the examples ahead have done their homework. They build innovative learning experiences on sound instructional strategies, emphasizing inquiry, collaboration, and active engagement. Even projects that appear playful involve learning goals that are absolutely serious, with assessment strategies that look critically at what students know and can do. Across grade levels and subjects, students who are learning to innovate move through a process that teaches them how to frame problems, generate ideas, refine solutions, collaborate with peers and experts, and share results. (We'll unpack specific skills that emerge through this process in future chapters.) In designing these 21st century learning experiences, educators exhibit many of the qualities associated with innovators from other fields.

Your Innovation Profile

Whether innovators are drumming up new business ideas or hard at work solving community problems, they share certain characteristics. They tend to be action-oriented. They know how to network. They're willing to take calculated risks. They look ahead, anticipating benefits that others might not have imagined yet. They work to overcome obstacles. Especially in the social sector, they're generous about sharing what they know and eager to help good ideas grow. When educators exhibit these qualities, they show students how innovators think and act. They become innovation role models.

Let's take a closer look at these qualities. If you're a teacher looking for opportunities to bring innovation into the classroom, start by considering your own strengths and weaknesses as an innovator. If you're a school leader, consider how you encourage—or discourage—innovation among your staff. In the chapters ahead, as you learn more about innovators from diverse fields, be on the lookout for strategies that will increase your ability to think creatively and inspire more innovation among your colleagues. That's going to set the stage for your students to become more confident, capable innovators.

Are You Action Oriented?

Taking action is a hallmark of innovators. It's equally true whether you're talking about educators developing new projects or social entrepreneurs implementing life-saving approaches to health care. Stanford University's d.school, a global hotbed of design thinking and innovation, calls this trait a "bias toward action." It's about "doing and making over thinking and meeting" (d.school, 2010, p. iii).

In the classroom, a take-action teacher recognizes opportunities. This is the kind of educator, like Michael Thornton, whose attitude is, "I can do something with this."

Do You Know How to Network?

Educators who are determined to unleash their students' innovative capacities show another common characteristic. They are eager to share. They know how to network. Using Web 2.0 tools, many of today's innovative teachers and school leaders are thinking aloud about what's working and what's hard in their classrooms and communities. Their blogs, tweets, and wikis open a window on ideas at the formative stage. Their thoughtful reflections also allow others to learn from their examples and build on their insights, demonstrating the power of social networks to grow good ideas.

Educators who know how to network take part in online and in-person communities to advance their professional learning.

Are You Willing to Take Risks?

It may feel risky to learn in public, but educators who take this approach are modeling what it means to be a risk-taker—another known quality of innovators. Educators who are risk-takers are likely to be applying for grants or accessing resources in other creative ways, piloting new instructional approaches, or challenging policies that limit students' ability to learn.

Can You Look Ahead?

Here's the tricky part about innovation: it's hard to see it coming. Once an innovative idea or product has taken hold, it's difficult to imagine doing without it. (Can you recall a time before seat belts or smartphones?) Because innovation creates a new normal, it's often only in hindsight that we can see the wisdom of breakthrough ideas.

The challenge comes at the early stage, when it's tempting to dismiss novel ideas as impractical or impossible. Glen Bull, an education professor at University of Virginia, emphasizes the importance of looking ahead so you can position yourself to catch the early wave of a promising classroom strategy or emerging technology. This is part of the innovator's mindset too. In the 1990s, Bull's forward thinking helped get schools connected to the Internet. Although many of today's teachers and students would be hard-pressed to remember a time before schools had access to this online world, the Internet was once an untested, even controversial idea for education. "When we first proposed connecting all public schools to the Internet, people thought that was the craziest thing they'd ever heard of," Bull admits. "What people missed seeing was the trajectory—imagining where this could go. You have to consciously link [innovations] to learning outcomes."

Now, Bull and his team are hard at work on a new project that introduces children to engineering with the use of inexpensive desktop fabricators—a kind of 3-D printer. The idea is in the pilot stages (and gets a full discussion in chapter 7). Although the details are still being tested and refined, Bull can imagine what this approach might eventually accomplish in terms of engaging learners and deepening their understanding of math and science. "We're right at the cusp," he says, "in the same way that we caught the leading edge of the Internet revolution. We expect this to be just as profound."

Educators who know how to look ahead are able to anticipate the benefits of introducing promising approaches or technologies.

Can You Overcome Obstacles?

Innovation can be a messy process, fraught with failure and frustration. Even in the business world, where there's tolerance for risk if it might lead to financial rewards, the quest for new ideas can result in "the mess, the conflict, failure, emotions, and looping circularity that is part and parcel of the creative process," acknowledges Bruce Nussbaum, an innovation expert who teaches a class called Design at the Edge at Parsons The New School for Design (Nussbaum, 2011). If we can accept the creative mess that comes along with the process, innovation stands a chance. That's hard enough for corporate managers to tolerate. The challenge looms larger in education, where there's little tolerance for wrong answers or messy learning.

Educators who have the innovator's mindset don't get frustrated by "yeah, but . . ." thinking. They find work-arounds to obstacles, whether that means being creative about securing resources, finding flexibility within the curriculum, or overcoming technology barriers so that students have access to the powerful tools they need.

Do You Help Good Ideas Grow?

Innovative educators find a way to move ideas ahead. They not only recognize opportunities, but also know how to create them. And once they hit on a good idea, they make sure to spread the word. Being able to take a worthy idea to scale is one more quality that innovators share.

Educators with this mindset know how to build buzz for good ideas. They find allies and brainstorming partners. They build collaborative platforms, such as project wikis that others can join and expand. They open windows to the innovation happening in their classroom by inviting the community to project showcase events or posting video documentaries of student accomplishments.

When these qualities come together in the classroom, students stand to gain. Antero Garcia offers a good example. A high school English teacher in a high-poverty neighborhood of Los Angeles, he regularly designs learning experiences that engage students in new ways (we'll hear later about the alternate reality games and other digital media experiences that give his students a greater sense of agency as learners). These experiences unfold because he stays on the lookout for connections and expertise beyond the classroom. He looks for opportunities in which students can influence their community. He reflects publicly about these projects on his blog, The American Crawl, as well as on collaborative publishing sites like the National Writing Project's *Digital Is*.

Embracing the role of innovator may mean taking on more work and more risk as a teacher. But it's a label that Garcia and others who share his outlook find refreshing. "*Innovation* is not a word you hear much in teaching circles or as a way to describe what teachers do. In my experience as a teacher," he says, "no one's ever called us innovators." The very word "sounds disruptive," he adds, but in a good way. "If used authentically by the teaching profession, innovation could be a way to turn things around."

Imagine the energy we might unleash if we can encourage more of these qualities, among educators and students alike.

Borrow This Idea

When Michael Thornton thinks about the ideal learning environment for encouraging good thinkers, he pictures an Apple store. "The tools are out in the open, ready to use. Everyone can see what other people are doing. No one hesitates to walk up to someone else and ask, how did you do that? That's what I want my classroom to feel like."

To duplicate that energizing vibe, he started experimenting with the physical layout of his classroom. Every couple weeks, he would rearrange the furniture and watch what happened. Eventually, a student asked what was going on. That question generated a class conversation about the learning environment. How would students choose to redesign the space so that it would encourage their best thinking? What could they change without spending any money on new furniture? Where should the existing technology go?

Those questions led to an action research project. Students drew scale-model plans on graph paper for their proposed classroom redesigns. That gave them practice visually representing their thinking and also sparked conversations about what makes for a good schematic. (Hint: labels help.) Students also had to explain their rationale. "I want them to be able to tell me why," Thornton says.

This wasn't a theoretical exercise. Every week, they would test another plan and evaluate the impact on learning. They discussed what worked well, what didn't, what was feasible, what was impossible (such as one student's request for a shark tank). By the end of the school year,

Thornton was drawing on students' observations about collaboration to support his request for circular tables to replace individual desks.

In many ways, this was a low-stakes project that required little class time. There were some connections to standards, such as measurement and scale in mathematics, but the big idea was to give students more voice in shaping their learning experience. "Just the idea that this is their room—that's a new concept for them," Thornton reflects. "You should have seen the look in their eyes when they realized we were actually going to test their plans. They need to know that they can play a part in what happens at school." By the end of the project, Thornton saw a shift in attitude. Students were more apt to make suggestions and initiate the use of classroom technologies, such as interactive boards or document cameras, to share their thinking. "They understand now that this is their stuff," he adds, "not mine."

In a similar project, fifth graders at the National Inventors Hall of Fame School in Akron, Ohio, set out to tackle the issue of reducing noise in their school library. Their efforts follow the classic arc of project-based learning: starting with a compelling, open-ended question ("How can we make our library quieter?"), learning through research ("How does sound travel?"), brainstorming solutions (from more obvious ones, like using drapes or kites to baffle sound, to more creative ones, like installing a noise-buffering aquarium in the wall), improving through teamwork, developing a final product, and finally, presenting scale models to an authentic audience (Bronson & Merryman, 2010).

Borrow from these ideas to develop an innovation exercise that asks students to describe their ideal learning environment. Throughout the exercise, emphasize key thinking strategies (italicized in the following text and explained in more detail in upcoming chapters).

To jump-start their creativity, encourage students to *think in metaphors*. Would they like school to feel more like an Apple store? Video game? Workshop? Art studio? What does that mean?

Have them *brainstorm in small groups* about what they might do now—without spending a dime—to transform the space where they come together to engage in learning and thinking. Can they *identify problems* with the existing space?

Move from theory to practice by having students *test their plans* and ask students to *reflect on results*. This will offer an opportunity for students to *think critically* about what worked well, what didn't, and why.

Chapter 3

Growing a New Global Skill Set

Veteran teacher Michael Baer has always made an effort to connect what his students are learning in the classroom to the real world. But even thirty-five years in education didn't prepare him for the powerful learning that would unfold when he agreed to help students from the small town of Berne, Indiana, figure out how they could get clean drinking water to the people of Haiti.

Their project would grow to engage the entire K–12 school district and community of five thousand. It would test students' and teachers' capacity to be problem solvers and take them face-to-face with the worst poverty in the Western Hemisphere. It would stretch students' communication skills and challenge them to use digital media for an important purpose.

Students who were part of this project, called Dots in Blue Water, learned what it means to live in an interconnected world. They acquired a new set of skills for tackling difficult problems and became impassioned advocates for a cause they cared about. Their experience offers a compelling case study of innovative, 21st century learning.

Baer's students used a problem-solving process that echoes the way innovators work in many fields and that corresponds with the stages of project-based learning. As a classroom process, it's content neutral. That means it's equally adaptable for projects involving math or science, creative writing or visual arts, digital media, or any number of interdisciplinary areas. Throughout this process, a variety of important activities and thinking patterns come into play (see table 3.1, page 38).

Many of the classroom activities outlined in table 3.1 will be familiar to teachers who already engage in project-based learning and other forms of inquiry-based instruction. However, we all know that not every project leads to innovation. Let's take a closer look at Dots in Blue Water to see how classroom decisions and learning activities helped students achieve their remarkable success. Later in the chapter, we'll suggest additional practices to build your students' innovation skills.

Table 3.1: Innovative Learning Process

Process	What Students Are Doing	How Teacher Supports Them
Frame problems	Researching to identify root causes of issues, finding right-sized problems, understanding multiple perspectives	Crafting a driving question or design brief to frame problem, ensuring students have a need to know, aligning project with core academic content, incorporating student voice and choice, building empathy
Generate solutions	Brainstorming, borrowing, adapting, or improving on existing ideas, seeking inspiration from unexpected sources	Asking questions to encourage in-depth inquiry, encouraging risk-taking, modeling brainstorming strategies
Refine ideas	Engaging in iterative cycles of prototyping, testing, getting feedback, reflecting, evaluating, revising	Allowing for multiple cycles of review and revision, providing timely feedback, encouraging learning from failure
Engage with others	Collaborating with team members, networking with broader audience, engaging with experts	Encouraging effective collaboration skills, helping students identify and connect with experts outside the classroom
Share results	Communicating through various media, advocating, inspiring others to grow worthy ideas	Conducting authentic assessment, inviting public audience, encouraging reflection

Welcome Authentic Questions

Dots in Blue Water began with a compelling question. On an otherwise ordinary day in late 2009, Baer was explaining to a class of sophomores at South Adams High how poor environmental decisions had contributed to humanitarian catastrophes in Haiti. By coincidence, a friend of Baer's happens to be headmaster at a small rural school that sits in the flood plain outside of Port-au-Prince. Over the years, trees were stripped from this landscape and sold for quick profits. Without vegetation, topsoil eroded. When three hurricanes hit the Caribbean island in quick succession, raging flood waters rolled right up to the schoolhouse doors. An email from the headmaster described how students scrambled onto the roof to try to survive, even though they were without food or clean drinking water. Many perished.

"I'm telling my students, this is why you don't strip off the vegetation," Baer recalls. "This is why you take care of your environment. It's why we study earth science." A number of system failures contributed to this tragedy, but it was the lack of access to clean drinking water—something many people take for granted—that caught the attention of one of Baer's students. She raised her hand and said, "We do all these science labs to learn stuff. Why can't we do a lab and help these people figure out how to purify their water?"

For Baer, that question marks a profound before-and-after point in his teaching career. "This was one of those redefining moments," he says. "I knew that answering her question could redefine who we are as teachers, as students, as a school. I said to her, let's make that happen."

Good projects start with good questions. Baer took his student's curiosity seriously enough to use it as the jumping-off point for a new project. The student was asking for relevance; she wanted to apply science content to an authentic problem. She was also posing an open-ended inquiry. There's more than one possible solution to her question about how to purify water for people in a low-resource environment. To answer it, students would need to *frame the problem* through research and brainstorm possible solutions to evaluate as a team. It had the makings of a great project, setting the stage for innovative thinking.

It was up to Baer to make sure that investigating this question would also lead students to important learning goals. With approval from his administration and clear connections to science standards, he adjusted his lesson plans so that students could spend every Friday on their new project. Eventually, the project would expand to address standards across a number of content areas, including social studies, language arts, math, and digital media.

Encourage Effective Teamwork

To tackle this complex problem, Baer's students organized themselves into teams according to their interests. Teamwork wasn't a contrived part of this project; it was essential for breaking a big, openended question into manageable pieces.

One team focused on research, investigating questions that the larger group raised and applying information literacy skills. "We knew there would be a lot of questions," Baer says. "For example, what's causing the water to be unsafe to drink? When we started, none of us knew much about Haiti's environment." Exploring underlying causes of water contamination helped frame the problem, so that students knew they were working on the most appropriate solutions.

Another team appealed to students "who were more hands-on tinkerers," Baer says. "They were our development group." Their charge was to strategize and experiment with best methods for purifying water, applying the same problem-solving processes that engineers use.

Recognizing that many others have explored the problem of water purification, students looked beyond the classroom for experts willing to share their insights. They found a retired Indiana engineer who had patented a water purification device. He gave them a prototype and permission to work with it. They began taking it apart, testing the electrolysis device with different salts and voltages, and making adjustments to improve the efficiency. From this, students learned the value of prototyping and revising to achieve results. They also discovered that innovation can mean improving on someone else's ideas rather than inventing from scratch. "I told them, this may not be our invention, but it will certainly have our fingerprints all over it," Baer says.

Meanwhile, another team worked on marketing and promotional materials, using writing and digital-technology skills for an authentic purpose. A key moment for the marketing team unfolded when a student found an essay by nature writer Annie Dillard. In it, Dillard described her then-seven-year-old daughter's response to hearing about a deadly tsunami. The child suggested that the lives lost to drowning would look like "dots in blue water." That poignant metaphor grabbed the attention of Baer's students and became the project brand.

A fourth team took on the task of community investing, applying concepts from math and finance. "We didn't want to call it fundraising," the teacher explains. "That sounds like, if you give us money, we'll go away.

We wanted people to know they were investing, not only in the work in Haiti, but truly investing in what is locally going on in our classrooms."

Each Friday, students would push together their classroom desks "so it looked like the boardroom table in Donald Trump's *The Apprentice*," Baer says. Instead of the cutthroat competition that the show inspires among contestants, however, this project gave students opportunities to practice genuine collaboration. Teams took turns presenting results from their week's investigations, teaching each other what they had learned and encouraging group problem solving. New questions that emerged from this process were referred to the research team, who did their best to find answers by the following Friday.

As South Adams students discovered, inspiration may start with an individual spark, but moving forward with an idea often requires a team effort. Researchers Anita Woolley and Thomas Malone understand the value of teamwork. Their studies show that teams are "smarter" than the sum of their individual members. Here's how Woolley deconstructs the benefits of teams:

> What do you hear about great groups? Not that the members are all really smart but that they listen to each other. They share criticism constructively. They have open minds. They're not autocratic. And in our study we saw pretty clearly that groups that had smart people dominating the conversation were not very intelligent groups. (Woolley & Malone, 2011, p. 32)

Be Ready to Go Big

As the project moved from research to real-life application, interest grew. Initially, participants consisted of about thirty students from two sections of an integrated chemistry and physics class. Then the 2010 earthquake struck Haiti, and the need for clean drinking water became even more acute. More students got interested in joining the project. Baer asked his superintendent about turning Dots in Blue Water into a schoolwide effort. "His eyes lit up," the teacher recalls, and the project scope changed again.

Innovators have a tendency to think big. They're eager to help good ideas spread widely. By expanding this project, more students gained the chance to contribute to something meaningful. Their shared efforts yielded even greater results when their story engaged the wider community.

Throughout the 2010–11 school year, every student in South Adams Schools became part of this authentic, interdisciplinary learning experience. Kindergartners learned about the importance of clean hands and hygiene. Music students studied Caribbean rhythms. In art classes, students learned about the folk artists of the region. "The entire school community wrapped its arms around Dots in Blue Water. Every teacher found a way to tie in a curriculum focus on water purification or Haiti," Baer says.

Students used their communication skills to engage with an even larger audience. South Adams High students were often in the role of teaching younger students and adult community groups about water purification and conservation issues. Using social media, they spread the word about Dots in Blue Water. By June 2011, they had raised $43,000 from the local community.

Culminating activities are important to cement learning in project-based learning, and this project exceeded expectations at this stage as well. In June 2011, eight students selected through a competitive application process set off for Haiti, accompanied by eight teachers. They brought along five purification devices. The team of student tinkerers had made improvements so that a single device could purify fifty-five gallons of water per minute, powered by a 12-volt battery. An engineering consultant who accompanied the South Adams contingent to Haiti was so impressed by one student's schematics that he asked to borrow the plans for future installations.

During a life-changing week in Haiti, students installed the devices and taught Haitians how to maintain equipment so that villagers would have a sustainable source of clean water. One system brought clean water to the same school that had suffered losses during earlier flooding. Another was installed in a nearby village about the size of Berne, Indiana.

While students were trying to decide where to install their last three devices, news broke about a cholera outbreak in a mountain village of about one thousand. Some three hundred people were already ill. "We realized cholera could wipe out the whole village," Baer says. Quickly, the team decided to send its last device there. Five teachers made the arduous trek while South Adams students stayed behind for safety reasons. Once the three-tank system was in place, the village experienced no new outbreaks of cholera.

Baer doesn't have to look far to see the impact of this project. Four of the students who traveled to Haiti were graduating seniors. One of them is the student who first asked about how they might help the people of Haiti. She's now off to college, studying to be a nurse in the developing world. Another recent graduate, who worked on social media and made video documentaries about the trip, is preparing for a career as a foreign correspondent. "Our lives were changed forever by this," she says. Baer also has seven teacher colleagues who saw firsthand how students can make a real difference in their world.

"Everybody has taken a step higher," he says. "Our entire school community has a new attitude. We're not going to stand idly by and let somebody else fix the problems of the world."

Incorporate Further Key Practices

It's a rare project that achieves the life-saving impact of Dots in Blue Water. Yet the same strategies that made it effective can be incorporated into smaller-scale projects. To foster innovation, teachers can follow Baer's lead and be on the lookout for opportunities to encourage authentic inquiry, effective teamwork, and big thinking about what students can accomplish. They can also incorporate more practices—often used by innovators outside the classroom—to encourage better thinking and problem solving.

Build Empathy

Innovation doesn't happen in a vacuum. Innovators who have empathy can step outside their own perspective and see issues from multiple viewpoints. Approaching a problem in this way can lead to better solutions. That's why professional designers often conduct ethnographic studies to understand the needs of specific user groups in different contexts. It's also why the Stanford d.school incorporates empathy-building activities into its design thinking processes for K–12 schools.

To see how empathy leads to better solutions, let's hear from a social innovator named Thorkil Sonne. He is a former telecom executive from Denmark who established a company called Specialisterne, Danish for "the specialists." This social enterprise places people with autism in quality-control jobs for some of the world's largest technology companies, which pay competitive rates to contract with skilled software testers.

Sonne's motivation to create new opportunities for people with autism is intensely personal. His youngest child was diagnosed with autism as a preschooler. At first, Sonne and his wife scoured the research literature, looking for information that would give them hope about their son's future. They found only "documented despair." Research suggested his young son faced a likelihood of bullying and social isolation in childhood and lack of meaningful work as an adult. Frustrated, Sonne decided to get to know some people with autism to get a better picture of what was in store for his son. The adolescents and young adults he met through organizations serving the autism community "were really nice guys, and so good with their computers. They knew corners of the Internet I didn't know existed. They were so trustworthy and straightforward." Yet, he met no one with autism employed in a job that made good use of these skills.

From his own experience, Sonne knew that many technology companies struggle to fill quality-control jobs, which often involve repetitive tasks and require an extreme eye for detail. He says, "I got the feeling that these guys could be wonderful software testers." Sonne set up Specialisterne "as a company where people with autism are the normal ones." Employees typically fall on the high-functioning end of autism spectrum disorders. They may lack social skills, but in this business context, that's not a hindrance. "They don't have to be flexible, team players. We'll take care of that, and they can just do what they're good at," Sonne explains. By 2011, Specialisterne was generating about $3 million in annual revenues and had plans to expand around the globe.

In the classroom, teachers can encourage empathy through activities that ask students to deliberately consider issues from others' points of view. For the Dots in Blue Water project, students researched the day-to-day realities of people living in rural Haiti to understand why so many residents there lack access to clean water. With that understanding, they were better able to imagine practical solutions, such as providing purified water at a school or in a central place in a village. Similarly, for Studio H students in North Carolina, developing a farmers' market involved interviewing local farm families to understand their business needs and market limitations.

Empathy-building strategies don't have to be limited to full-fledged projects. On a regular basis, teachers across grade levels can encourage students to develop the habits of being observant, asking questions, considering multiple perspectives, and challenging preconceptions. At the Stanford d.school, empathy-building exercises involve drawing inferences based on observations. For example, students might observe children at a playground and make inferences about why they use or avoid specific games. In the classroom, a teacher might ask students to offer hunches about why people behave the way they do in specific contexts, such as current events, historical contexts, films, or works of literature.

More empathy-building activities include:

- Making field observations or shadowing people immersed in an issue or problem

- Conducting user interviews or focus groups to uncover diverse perspectives

- Taking part in role plays, in which students take on another person's point of view (for example, while studying a work of literature or a period in history)

- Inviting guest speakers to share their understanding of a particular issue or perspective

- Helping students connect with those from outside their peer group (for example, having children interview elders about their life experiences, having teens plan literacy or math activities for preschoolers, or using technology to connect with people from other cultures or countries)

- Gathering stories or artifacts that offer insights into what someone is thinking

Building empathy offers benefits that go beyond innovative thinking. Schools that emphasize social and emotional learning to foster positive school climate make a habit of incorporating activities that build awareness of others' emotions and perspectives.

Uncover Passion

As we've heard repeatedly, innovators are passionate about their ideas. That's what keeps them motivated to persist despite long odds and flawed first efforts. Peter Senge, director of the Center for Organizational Learning at MIT Sloan School of Management, puts it this way: "Innovators innovate because there is something they are passionate about" (Scanlon, 2008).

Helping students discover their passions is a critical step in the process of encouraging innovative thinking. To connect classroom projects with issues students care about, educators might want to find out what drives student interest during out-of-school time. A classroom survey could ask students: When you feel most creative, what are you doing? Where are you? What tools or technologies are you using? Their answers should offer insights into students' interests, setting the stage for more engaging projects.

"Student voice and choice" is an essential component of project design, according to project-based learning experts at the Buck Institute for Education. Teachers can bring more student voice into projects by paying attention to topics that generate classroom buzz. English teacher Shelley Wright, a thoughtful edublogger, describes how her high school students responded to reading *Sold*, a contemporary novel about a girl who was trafficked. First, students conducted research to help frame the problem of slavery in contemporary society. Wright describes what followed this initial inquiry phase:

> After researching, we come back together to discuss what needs to happen next. What is the best way to present our learning? What will be the most powerful? What do we want others to learn from us? Throughout this process, my students do most of the talking and leading. I tend to sit and listen, and at critical moments, draw out the nuances or similarities of what is being said. And when things aren't working, sometimes I need to suggest a new direction. (Wright, 2011)

Her students chose to lead a social media campaign to teach others about modern-day slavery. It's a difficult, gritty topic. But the project meets important learning standards, including using social media wisely and communicating for an authentic purpose. What's more, it meets Wright's goal for her students: "It's not enough for my students to learn about slavery; they need to do something with the knowledge, specifically 'real-world' projects that matter" (Wright, 2011).

Students can also benefit from listening to adults who are passionate about their work. Innovators tend to be eloquent spokespersons for the causes they care about. Teachers can connect students with them by inviting guest speakers or arranging Skype chats, planning field trips, or assigning students to critique readings or videos that capture the distinct voices of innovators. (See appendix A, page 135, for resource suggestions.)

Amplify Worthy Ideas

Just as viable ideas can originate anywhere in today's networked world, opportunities to provide essential support are also getting flattened. Philanthropy and venture funding, once reserved for the wealthy, have been crowdsourced with online platforms like Kiva (an online microlending platform to support entrepreneurs in the developing world) and Kickstarter, the crowdsourcing marketplace for creative ideas we heard about earlier. That means there are more opportunities than ever to help grow an idea if you have the wisdom to spot it.

To participate in the culture of innovation, students need to be able to do more than generate their own ideas. They also need to know how to critically evaluate others' brainstorms and decide which ones are worth supporting. When they see the kernel of a worthy idea from any corner of the globe, they need to know how to provide essential support to help it grow. Being savvy about social media can help promising projects go viral. As we saw in Dots in Blue Water, knowing how to nurture, grow, and advocate for ideas is part of innovative thinking, too.

Meg Wirth is someone who understands how to be an amplifier for other people's good thinking. She founded an online global marketplace called Maternova, which aims to accelerate innovation in the field of maternal and neonatal health. The focus is on improving the health of mothers and newborns in parts of the world where medical care and supplies are lacking, making pregnancy a leading cause of death for women of childbearing age.

The problem isn't a lack of creative problem solving to improve the health of low-income populations; it's often a lack of connections. Good ideas are abundant. Many low-cost solutions for the developing world are coming from Western schools of engineering, public health, medicine, and even business, as students from these disciplines focus on causes they care about. Equally ingenious ideas are emerging from some of the world's distressed villages and urban slums. "These are places where health care providers have had to improvise, devise workarounds, and come up with novel ideas," Wirth explains. For example, the "bambulance" is a bicycle-pulled emergency medical transport device designed in Kenya. Made of bamboo, it's lightweight and strong, and can go places where motorized ambulances are either unavailable or impractical. Another low-tech product, a mat that measures blood loss, helps midwives detect postpartum hemorrhage, a leading—and preventable—cause of maternal death.

Yet despite their resourcefulness, innovators from the developing world often lack the connections and capital to turn their good ideas into viable products that can be mass produced. That's why a colleague like Wirth, based in Rhode Island, is helpful for connecting them with a larger global community. Maternova aims to accelerate the spread of good ideas by tracking down "the lifesaving innovations that could change everything," Wirth explains, and then using the Internet to broadcast that information. The online platform also sparks conversations and gathers helpful feedback from users. That feedback, in turn, informs product design and leads to more improvements and new product development. Maternova offers a window on innovation as an ongoing, iterative, collaborative process. "We've only seen the tip of the iceberg," Wirth promises.

Translating this kind of thinking to the classroom could mean having students evaluate a number of team proposals before deciding which one to develop further. Evaluation of each other's ideas gives students an opportunity to apply critical thinking. They may decide to throw their collective energy behind one idea or pull components from multiple projects into a final project.

Know When to Say No

Being a critical thinker also means being able to spot ideas that aren't ready for prime time. Bold new ideas may have bugs that need to be worked out. An approach that appears to be a game-changer may be too expensive for the benefits it affords or may have unanticipated consequences. Give students opportunities to look for potential pitfalls and to know when to say no.

PlayPumps, for instance, looked like a winner. It's a merry-go-round for kids that doubles as a water pump. With each turn, more ground water is pumped into an above-ground storage tank. This elegantly simple solution to deliver clean drinking water in the developing world proved irresistible. In 2000, the idea won a World Bank Developmental Marketplace competition, which included $165,000 in prize money to install PlayPumps in South Africa. At the Clinton Global Initiative in 2006, former President Bill Clinton and then First Lady Laura Bush announced another $16 million in support. Even music celebrities like Jay-Z got on board, raising money and awareness with a benefit concert and documentary.

But however charming the concept, PlayPumps was running into problems in implementation. A UNICEF evaluation found that children did not play often enough to keep the water tanks filled. That left it up to village women in Mozambique and elsewhere to keep the merry-go-rounds turning. More negative engineering reports led to press critiques of PlayPumps as "too expensive, too complex for local maintenance, over-reliant on child labor, and based on flawed water demand calculations" (Chambers, 2009).

By 2010, philanthropist Jean Case wrote about "the painful acknowledgment of coming up short" and announced that PlayPumps was being folded into an organization called Water for People, which offers a portfolio of technologies to address water issues. She was also forthcoming about the challenge of saying *no* when it comes to investing in an innovative idea:

> Turns out innovating is hard work anywhere and anytime. In the developing world even more so. But if the philanthropic sector is transparent about mistakes and lessons along the way, and adapts as the situation calls for, hopefully we'll all end up a little wiser and a little closer to solutions that can more effectively address the daunting challenges of our day. (Case, 2010)

Helping students learn from failure is a key strategy for innovation (which you'll hear more about in chapter 7). In classrooms that emphasize the process of innovating, students have freedom to test ideas without fear of failure. Their investigations uncover what works as well as what doesn't. Both kinds of information are important to innovators. As a nonprofit leader told me, "Finding out what doesn't work lets us cross things off the whiteboard."

Encourage Breakthroughs

In project-based learning, assessment plans typically evaluate 21st century skills such as collaboration, problem solving, and creativity, along with mastery of important content knowledge. Thom Markham, an advocate for project-based learning, encourages teachers to add a category called "breakthrough" to project rubrics. He explains his thinking in this blog post:

> It's not the 'A' category—that's Mastery or Commended or a similar high-ranking indicator. The breakthrough column goes beyond the A, rewarding innovation, creativity, and

something new outside the formal curriculum. It's a 'show me' category. Students like it, and so do teachers. It particularly appeals to high-end students who feel current offerings are drab, or to the middling student who will not work just for a grade, but who seeks the psychic reward of creating something cool. (Markham, 2010)

Before adding a breakthrough category to project rubrics, teachers need to think about how they will recognize this level of performance. What would students need to make, do, or show to demonstrate breakthrough proficiency? How will you know a breakthrough when you see it? Talking with experts from your discipline will help you gather examples from real life that show what it means to reach a breakthrough solution to a difficult problem. Students need to understand that they shouldn't expect to reach this level of achievement with every project. Breakthroughs are indeed rare—but are also worth recognizing and celebrating when they occur.

Borrow This Idea

To give his students authentic practice as global decision makers, Bill Ferriter started a Kiva Club with his middle schoolers in North Carolina. Using investment dollars that students raised through their own creative efforts, the club invests in microloans for small-scale entrepreneurs in the developing world. Although some high school students run Kiva Clubs as extracurricular activities, Ferriter has found countless ways to connect this motivating project to the standards-based curriculum. Students learn about social studies by understanding what life is like for real people. They use rubrics to evaluate potential loans and balance their portfolio to include lenders in dozens of countries on nearly every continent. They compare interest rates that borrowers are charged. They make persuasive speeches to their classmates about individual entrepreneurs they find compelling, along with videos to advertise their efforts and maps to track the real change they are making in the world.

The project builds students' empathy by exposing them to the personal stories of entrepreneurs from other countries. It allows students to practice making evaluations, using their critical thinking for an authentic purpose. It also challenges them to make a case for ideas they care about and to know when to say no. As part of a connected community of changemakers, students in the Kiva Club are learning firsthand what it means to take action.

Part II

Building the New Idea Factory

In hot spots across the country, pioneering educators are making innovation a priority. Schools engaged in this exciting work offer us a research and development lab for figuring out how to teach about innovation. Some are introducing their students to design thinking, a deliberate framework for problem solving, which we've been hearing about in previous chapters. Others are giving students a chance to think like engineers or influence their communities through games that have real-world implications.

As we take a closer look at these schools and classrooms in the following case studies, put on your own critical lenses and consider: Which ideas are you ready to borrow now? What seems possible longer term? What feels out of reach in your current situation (and why)? Each case study ends with practical suggestions for how to get started.

Interspersed with these examples are five Strategy Spotlights to further expand your innovation toolkit. Inspired by the work that innovators do outside the classroom, these strategies have ready applications to the world of teaching and learning. By bringing more of these strategies to school, you can start to build a new idea factory that meets the needs of today's learners.

Chapter 4

Seeding Innovation

As we've seen, innovative ideas can come from any corner of the globe. Rather than waiting for good ideas to emerge as if by magic, one district is making a deliberate effort to seed innovation. In the following example, watch how a clear vision of innovative learning sets the stage for deliberate action steps.

Pam Moran, superintendent of Albemarle County Public Schools, is no newcomer to education. During her twenty-five years with the Virginia district, she has moved from the classroom to administration without losing her youthful enthusiasm or curiosity. Her mobile device is always handy so that she can tweet and blog her way through each day. "She may have white hair," a longtime colleague says, "but at heart she's a multitasker, just like our millennial students."

To give those thirteen thousand students a shot at a hopeful future, Moran is willing to challenge the comfort level of her adult colleagues. Whether she's speaking within her own district or as a national voice in education, Moran keeps her focus on "doing what's best for children. We need to transition from traditional schooling to a radically transformed vision of school. It's a big challenge," she admits. "We're doing a good job of what the state demands. But are we doing a good enough job for kids and teachers? We're not there yet."

Encourage Grassroots Ideas

This diverse district, covering 740 square miles at the foothills of the Blue Ridge Mountains, includes rural, urban, and suburban schools. You won't find a cookie-cutter approach to instruction or pacing guides to keep teachers tied to a standard curriculum. Instead, schools are encouraged to find their own identities as learning communities, whether that means emphasizing the arts or STEM, becoming a charter school, or adopting a project-based learning model like Expeditionary Learning. Technology use is strongly encouraged but not standardized. Students are free to bring their own digital devices, whatever they may be, and connect with the district's open network.

Students also advise administrators on whether any sites or tools should be restricted. "That's scary to some educators," Moran admits. "I've had teachers ask, what if students are playing [games like] Angry Birds? My answer is, well, then let's use it to teach math."

Encouraging innovation is a critical goal for Moran and her district. Figuring out how to make it happen has been a grassroots process. On the instructional side, she seeks to find the right balance between standards—which she considers necessary for providing a framework for the curriculum—and teacher creativity, which she also considers essential. When it comes to the functional tasks of the district, she looks to standardize where it makes sense "so that the business side of school runs smoothly."

One process the district uses to encourage out-of-the-box thinking is to award innovation seed grants. Any teacher with an idea worth pursuing—and a good rationale for suggesting it—can submit a proposal. Rather than looking for outside resources, the district reserves $100,000 in its budget to fund seed grants.

Becky Fisher, an administrator and former teacher who has been in the district almost as long as the superintendent, recalls that the grants began in 2002 as a way to encourage effective use of emerging technologies for 21st century teaching and learning. "The big goal was to get people out of silos. Proposals had to address inquiry, analysis, and reflection and involve an interdisciplinary team."

Initially, only a handful of proposals trickled in. Those first wish lists sounded surprisingly similar. Teachers wanted laptops for their own use and interactive whiteboards for their classrooms. Once those high-demand tools were piloted, they became standard equipment across the district. Last year, teachers and school leaders submitted $1 million worth of seed grant ideas, ranging from more flexible designs for classroom furniture to class sets of iPads. Only one-tenth of the requests could be funded with the district's pot of innovation dollars, but the exercise continues to be valuable for eliciting fresh ideas. "It's our R&D," Fisher says.

Indeed, this research-and-development approach feels more like the corporate world than the public education sector. "It's not money without strings," Fisher emphasizes. "There are deliverables. We want to be able to evaluate: what can we learn from this?" If there's a good idea in the mix but not enough money for it, the district may look for outside funding to give it a try.

Fisher, who wears several administrative hats (overseeing learning technologies, professional development, and media services for the district), is deliberate about following up on each grant. "How will we grow these seeds? What will we learn? What are the necessary follow-up steps?" She also knows that not every idea will work. Action research sometimes reveals what not to do again. She echoes a key innovation strategy when she asks, "How can we learn from small mistakes? The trick is making sure that the last one you made won't be your last opportunity to try something new."

Along with the innovation grants, the district also works closely with researchers at the University of Virginia. "We're an ideal test bed for them," says Fisher, who frequently makes her way to the office and innovation workshop of Professor Glen Bull in the Curry School of Education to brainstorm about emerging tools and technologies.

As a result of its various innovation efforts, Albemarle County Public Schools is working with teachers and school leaders to investigate a number of intriguing questions. Recent action research questions show how problems are being framed and suggest questions other districts might want to investigate:

- How can we teach children to solve problems using engineering?

- How can we leverage gaming and other high-interest activities to connect with students who are at risk of being disengaged from school?

- How can we use class sets of digital devices to expand learning opportunities for diverse students?

- How can we reimagine the school library as a media center and collaborative work space?

- How can we design school spaces and furnishings to foster student collaboration, research, and other activities necessary for project-based learning?

This may sound like a lot of experimenting, but it's a carefully managed risk. Fisher emphasizes the importance of starting small, paying attention to results, scaling success, and fostering a learning culture environment. Learning what not to do again is as important as taking good ideas to scale.

This environment attracts innovative thinkers. Chad Ratliff came to Albemarle County Public Schools to be the district's first assistant director of instruction and innovation projects. He brings credentials from both the education side (he's been both teacher and coach) and the business sector (he holds an MBA and has started small businesses that have a social purpose).

"I have an extremely high level of autonomy here. There's trust, distributed leadership—all these things we talk about as being best practices in educational leadership, they practice," Ratliff says. He looks to encourage innovative thinking among those who traditionally have had the least influence in school change: teachers and students. In most districts, he argues, top-down decision making is still the norm. Constraints are imposed by state and federal lawmakers, school boards, and district administrators. "The teacher and student are the two smallest voices," Ratliff says. He tries to turn that upside-down by going directly to teachers to find ideas worth testing. "I talk to teachers first. They have to be the drivers of innovation in the classroom, or they won't have ownership."

Like other innovators, Ratliff is prone to thinking in metaphors: "If the teacher is the entrepreneur, then the school leaders should take the role of venture capitalist to provide support and resources. The teacher needs to do the homework, to be able to say why an idea is worth investing in. Then it's up to me to go find resources. That's flipped from the model of me—as an administrator—telling you—a teacher—what to do, and then I might give you some money to help."

Like a discerning venture capitalist, Ratliff doesn't throw money at just any old idea. "When I review proposals, I look for measurability. And that doesn't have to mean a standardized, multiple-choice test. It's about impact. How will we know if an idea has made a difference? How does it fit what we're trying to accomplish? That's what we look for." This approach is more likely to help good ideas take hold, grow in scale, and be sustained. "Let's start with some small wins," Ratliff says, "then we can start expanding."

Seeding Ideas: How to Get Started

To start an innovation seed fund in your school or district, plan for:

- **Support**—Having even a modest amount of support dedicated to action research sends this pro-innovation message to teachers: we want your ideas.

- **Allies**—Recruit potential allies for your innovation efforts. In the Albemarle County Public Schools example, university partners play an important role. Local business advisers or nonprofit partners can be recruited to provide feedback, help evaluate projects, and plan for scaling results.

- **Selection**—Develop a smooth application process. Share judging criteria in advance. Be clear about big goals for seed ideas but open-ended about how teachers might accomplish them. Make the application process as streamlined and time efficient as possible.

- **Impact**—Decide how you will measure impact. Consider quantitative as well as qualitative indicators.

- **Results**—Create processes to ensure that you learn from failures as well as successes. Make sure good ideas get shared and replicated.

Strategy Spotlight: Be Opportunistic

At a glance: Innovators find opportunities in the most surprising places. They are hardwired to be resourceful.

When to use this strategy: To frame problems

If there's a superpower shared by today's innovators, it may be their ability to see opportunities where others see only problems or despair. They excel at reframing problems. Look around your community and you're likely to find examples of people who have managed to build something out of nothing. Discarded electronics become raw materials for teaching technology skills to those who have been on the wrong side of the digital divide. Broken bikes are used to teach disenfranchised youth about mechanical systems and empower them with personal transportation.

Such community programs make excellent field trips or places to recruit guest speakers who live and breathe frugal innovation. In hip-hop culture, this creative resourcefulness is known as *flipping something outta nothing*, according to *Hip Hop Genius* author Samuel Seidel. He cites examples such as satellite dishes made out of tin cans, old turntables powered by streetlamps, and vinyl tiles reborn as slick floors where new dance moves get invented. Learning to innovate with scarce resources is a skill worth encouraging. Seidel says, "How do you take what some consider trash and turn it into amazing things?"

Jeff Sturges and the Mt. Elliott Makerspace in Detroit offer a good example of being opportunistic. This community workshop operates outside the regular school structure and follows an informal learning approach. Makerspace gives youth access to inexpensive tools, such as soldering irons, wire cutters, simple screen-printing equipment, and various hand tools—the sorts of things that helped Sturges figure out how the world works back when he was a curious kid. Building materials come from the city's discards, such as broken bicycles and electronic junk.

The challenge for Makerspace participants is to make something new from these random parts. Or as Sturges puts it, "How can someone, at as young an age as possible, experiment with tools in a way that helps them learn, piques their interest and curiosity, and also allows them to address problems in their own neighborhood?" These are the young people, he predicts, who will lead Detroit's transition from Motor City to Maker City.

Sturges, whose community-building efforts have attracted foundation support, says the biggest untapped resource for the project is people. "We have so many retired people here with incredible skills! They have an ability to problem solve in ways that we need. What they know has value, and it's a resource you can find not only in Detroit and other Rust Belt cities, but in communities around the world."

Some innovators are able to turn homegrown ideas into national models. In 1990, a civil rights activist named Dorothy Stoneman noticed that East Harlem had two problems in abundance: housing in disrepair and youth at risk. She envisioned a way to turn these twin problems into a singular opportunity. Her solution: enable teens to gain job skills and complete their education while building affordable housing in their own neighborhood. YouthBuild now operates in forty-three states through a network of grassroots initiatives that have scaled this idea organically. YouthBuild is poised to grow even more dramatically by adding green-building methods to its repertoire—seizing on yet another opportunity.

In my hometown of Portland, Oregon, one of my favorite institutions is the ReBuilding Center, the largest nonprofit building materials reuse center in North America. Equal parts lumberyard, pack rat nest, and community meeting place, the ReBuilding Center keeps seven tons of construction debris out of the landfill every day. A workforce of fifty people sorts, prices, and eventually resells every donated door-knob, window frame, plumbing fixture, and length of lumber. The staff even deconstructs entire houses, taking them apart by hand so that everything from floorboards to ceiling insulation can be reused. While going about its Earth-friendly business, the ReBuilding Center also generates living-wage jobs, delivers workforce training, and strength-ens the fabric of this neighborhood on the rebound.

Covering a full city block, the ReBuilding Center has become such a well-known local landmark that it's easy to forget what it replaced. When Executive Director Shane Endicott was growing up in this neighborhood, his grandmother owned a tavern a stone's throw from where the ReBuilding Center stands today. He knew all the back-alley shortcuts, especially which ones to avoid. By the time he was in his early twenties, gang violence was so routine in this neighborhood that it was hard to get police to respond to a shooting.

Endicott is a natural collaborator. He started the ReBuilding Center with a few neighbors and a credit card advance (because no bank would give them a loan for their untested business idea). His own story is inseparable from the organization he founded and has nurtured for the past decade. "I'm about as unlikely a candidate for this role as you could imagine," he admits. His formal education stopped long before high school graduation, and he had no prior experience running a non-profit or managing a $3 million annual budget. His best preparation for a career in the recycling industry, he suspects, was growing up poor. "I was hard wired to be resourceful," he says.

Yet this soft-spoken social entrepreneur manages to see the symbol-ism in his situation. "At the ReBuilding Center, we take what society is planning to throw away," he explains, "and turn that liability into an asset." It's a formula that works equally well whether you're talking about salvaging construction materials or unleashing the potential of people who've had a rocky start in life.

It takes practice to develop the vision to see what's under your nose. But as Endicott often tells visitors at the ReBuilding Center, being able to find opportunities isn't a superpower. It's accessible to anyone will-ing to think differently. "If *I* could do this," he often says, "why can't you?"

The last time I visited the ReBuilding Center, Endicott was con-templating the space above the building and wondering what else they could build up there someday. Where others might see nothing but sky, he saw more opportunity. That seems like a great project starter for students. What could they dream up for their school rooftops?

Borrow This Idea

How can we leverage small things to accomplish big results? That's the driving question behind a service-learning project called the Penny Harvest, in which elementary and middle school students engage in philanthropy. The idea seems simple: students "harvest" a share of the pennies that all of us have stashed in our homes and use them to support local causes that they select. According to project founder Teddy Gross, America's idle pennies add up to a billion-dollar resource. What's more, pennies are an equal-opportunity resource. They collect in the homes and pockets of rich and poor alike.

Although the collection stage connects to standards in math (measurement, visual representation of data) and language arts (persuasive writing, public speaking), the project gets even more interesting once the harvest is done. That's when students form community roundtables and investigate local issues. After they select the issues they care about, they invite nonprofit organizations to apply for grants. This sets the stage for higher-order thinking, as students analyze which issues they want to support and then decide how to evaluate nonprofit applicants. Students often conduct interviews with nonprofit leaders, giving youth an opportunity to ask critical questions and use communication skills to engage with adults on an authentic task. The project typically concludes with student reflections, which are shared in digital stories, blogs, and other products.

Since the project started in 1991, students have harvested and donated more than $8 million to charitable causes. Visit the Penny Harvest website (www.commoncents.org) to learn more.

Chapter 5

Integrating Design Thinking Throughout the Curriculum

Standards-based instruction, already an expectation in schools across the country, has gained more traction with widespread adoption of the Common Core State Standards. Is there room for innovation within the standards-based curriculum? This example shows how one school network has found a solution—not by eliminating standards but by building a foundation for innovation that cuts across grade levels and subject areas.

From their first day of class until graduation, students who attend school in the Henry Ford Learning Institute network are immersed in the process of design thinking. The goal isn't necessarily to produce a new generation of designers. Rather, students learn a deliberate way of solving problems that emphasizes empathy along with creativity.

To see design thinking in action, I visit the newest school in the network. Henry Ford Academy: School for Creative Studies in Detroit's midtown cultural district shares a beautifully renovated historic building with its partner organization, the College for Creative Studies. In this urban setting, students from middle school through graduate school are part of a new kind of learning environment intended to help revive this struggling city through the power of innovation.

At capacity, some nine hundred middle and high school students will come from across Detroit to attend the academy. After opening its doors with a few grades in 2009, it has expanded to serve grades 6–12. Students share a roof—as well as cafeteria, state-of-the-art gym, and gleaming public spaces—with undergraduates and graduate students preparing for careers in the creative arts. Having teens rub elbows with not-too-much-older role models is no accident. In fact, everything about this institution—from the cutting-edge curriculum to the flexible, well-lighted learning studios—shows evidence of thoughtful design.

For students growing up in poverty in a city facing hard times, learning how to imagine better solutions is essential preparation for life. Although the school emphasizes readiness for college and careers and sets a goal of graduating 90 percent of students on time, "we also want students to become active agents in community redevelopment," explains Deborah Parizek. A founding teacher at the first Henry Ford Academy in nearby Dearborn, Michigan, Parizek now directs the Henry Ford Learning Institute (HFLI), which manages the four charter schools bearing the Henry Ford Academy brand.

Students don't necessarily show up at these schools equipped to fix the world's problems. "A lot of them arrive passive," Parizek admits, "and so we have to change that." Her observation reminds me of Emily Pilloton's comments about the students in the inaugural class of Studio H. The transition to more active learning doesn't happen overnight. Parizek and her colleagues have become adept at scaffolding students' experience with both tools and tips that support active learning. They are also deliberate about preparing teachers to facilitate the innovation process.

Parizek is no longer in the classroom on a regular basis, but she shares her practical insights during professional development sessions that get teachers ready to lead design challenges. I had a chance to sit in on a summer session, which Parizek and her HFLI colleagues cofacilitated with staff from the K–12 Lab at the Stanford d.school.

To get teachers comfortable with this new way of learning, professional development workshops take a full-immersion approach. That means teachers dive into the same activities that get students thinking in new ways. To take on the role of innovative problem solver, they go outside school and interact with community members to better understand what people think about local issues. They learn to build prototypes—fast—to make thinking visible so they can get feedback and improve ideas.

A typical activity for new students at HFLI schools—and for teachers during professional development—is to tackle a relatively simple design challenge with a tight timeline. For example: design an "ideal" school identification badge for a classmate. Designing someone else's name badge requires getting acquainted well enough to know something about the other person's likes and dislikes. It's a short-term, low-risk project, but there's more going on here than an icebreaker exercise. In the course of a class period, students move through a rapid-cycle process that introduces them to concepts like empathy, prototyping, and communicating their creative thinking with others. In condensed form, this is the same process that professionals use to understand and solve problems ranging from consumer challenges (how to improve the oral hygiene process) to international development issues (how to improve literacy rates for girls in the developing world).

When working with teachers, Parizek and colleagues model how to give crisp, clear explanations of the design process. An important early step, for example, is to build empathy for the user. That might unfold by conducting user interviews or doing field observations. Before students (or adults) head out to do this work in the community, they review tips for how to ask good questions and how to be a good listener. Parizek uses graphic organizers to help students focus their observations and take notes, and she encourages learners to keep track of their work in design notebooks. She checks for understanding with a quick "Cool?" Then she turns groups loose on the activity, modeling how to maintain high energy throughout the fast-paced design process.

Gradually, as students (and teachers) get familiar with this new way of thinking and doing, the design challenges become more complex and interdisciplinary. Students pursue in-depth learning during "deep dives" into problem solving that also tie to academic learning standards. They learn to approach problems with an attitude of "how might we . . . ?" Recent design challenges have explored: How might we reduce bullying in our community? How might we design an outdoor experience that appeals to people in our community? How might we ensure that our community has access to sufficient, healthy water?

During their years at an HFLI school, students learn to understand issues from multiple perspectives. They learn how to generate many ideas through deliberate methods and then evaluate and narrow the options through research, analysis, and collaboration. They understand how to make ideas visible by building prototypes, which can take a variety of forms (sketches, models, storyboards, even skits). They learn how to give and receive criticism, and understand what it means to fail fast en route to a better solution.

For designers and others who rely on being able to generate good ideas, brainstorming is too important to leave to chance. Students who attend schools in the Henry Ford Learning Institute network learn a process for "ideation" that's similar to the way professionals work at IDEO, a global design firm. Rules for better brainstorming remind them to:

- **Defer judgment**—Don't evaluate anything at this stage.

- **Encourage volume**—Let ideas flow.

- **Be visual**—Capture ideas in quick sketches.

- **Be succinct**—Summarize an idea with a one-line "headline."

- **Listen to others' ideas**—Share one at a time.

- **Build on others' ideas**—When you hear something you like (see previous suggestion), expand on it.

- **Encourage wild thinking**—Turn off the practicality filter and give imagination room to run.

Before launching into brainstorming, teachers intentionally "load" the experience by making sure students are clear about the topic. They pump up the energy level with warm-ups that get students on their feet, quickly exchanging ideas aloud. And once they start the actual brainstorming session, they make sure students capture every idea that emerges. One small-group session should elicit a sea of sticky notes. Students understand that this is a time for ideas to *flare* far and wide. Later, they will have time to *focus* on specific ideas they want to investigate or develop further.

If the flow of ideas starts to slow down, teachers can reengage students' creativity by asking questions like, "What would you do if you had a budget of $10 million?" Extreme funding changes the game by getting barriers out of the way and allowing impractical, blue-sky ideas to surface. Even impractical-sounding ideas may contain the germ of an idea that could be realized.

By their senior year, HFLI students are ready to tackle more independent challenges. To prepare for their Senior Mastery experience, they explore careers, develop a portfolio, write a résumé, and practice interviewing. Then it's up to them to line up a field experience, investing 75 to 100 hours in a career field they find interesting. No one sets up these experiences for them. Instead, students build confidence from having to cold-call local employers, find willing adult partners, and plan their research projects. Senior projects have taken students all over their communities, from working in museum archives to working in the morgue at a local hospital. One student landed a spot on a Ford engineering team and traveled to Toronto to help test prototypes of new braking systems. Finally, students present their research project findings and extensive written report to a defense committee. The whole experience is carefully thought out to build confidence along with competence, preparing students for their next steps as young adults.

Develop an Innovative Curriculum

It's taken time, fine-tuning, and risk-taking to develop the HFLI model. After launching the first Henry Ford Academy in Dearborn in 1997, the HFLI network gradually began to grow. With local community partnerships in place, the network opened new schools in San Antonio (HFA: Alameda School of Art and Design) and in Chicago (HFA: Powerhouse High). Before the newest campus opened in midtown Detroit, Parizek and colleagues wanted to take stock of lessons learned and challenges ahead. So they cold called David Kelley (just as they ask their students to cold call experts for advice). He's the founder of IDEO and a driving force behind Stanford's d.school.

Parizek recalls the conversation: "We talked with him about building an innovation-based learning community. The idea wasn't just to add a new class about creativity but to fundamentally reimagine school. How might we address the demand for graduates who are creative thinkers and innovative problem solvers? For us, that meant thinking about curriculum, student experiences, the physical space, how you interact with the community, how you acquire stuff and use money—everything. He thought that sounded exciting."

To tackle that sizeable challenge, HFLI and IDEO hosted a design workshop. About thirty people from across the country, with deep backgrounds in diverse fields, joined the conversation at the Henry Ford Museum. Two big questions were on the table:

1. If you could reimagine high school, what would it look like?

2. What should a high school graduate of the 21st century know and be able to do?

"From the ideas we heard," Parizek says, "we're still working, developing, thinking." Innovation—or, in this case, teaching and learning to innovate—is an ongoing process. Like a good designer, HFLI has cast a wide net for ideas, allowed for trial and error, conducted research and ongoing professional development, prompted reflection, and demonstrated a willingness to stretch beyond anyone's comfort level.

One of the outcomes of this process is the Foundations of Innovation curriculum, developed in collaboration by HFLI and the d.school's K–12 Lab. Now a signature program of all four schools in the network, the class is mandatory for incoming sixth and ninth graders. It's truly a foundation for the learning that comes next, across all disciplines.

Through hands-on experiences, students develop the following mind-sets that the d.school has identified as being core to design thinking.

- **Human centered:** Developing solutions in response to needs of a specific (human) user requires designers to develop empathy and "walk in the other's shoes."

- **Bias toward action:** Doing something is key to design thinking; without action, nothing happens.

- **Radical collaboration:** Cross-disciplinary thinking and collaboration with those who have different skill sets and talents is part of the process.

- **Culture of prototyping:** Rapid trials and a "fail fast" mentality are part of prototyping.

- **"Show, don't tell":** Designers need to be able to represent ideas—show their thinking—to gather feedback. This might mean communicating with a sketch, 3-D model, story, skit, or experience for the audience.

- **Mindful of process:** Designers cycle through this process, repeating steps as necessary to achieve a workable solution. The process works to their advantage, leading to better solutions. (d.school, 2010)

What do students gain from developing fluency as design thinkers? Their work speaks volumes. For example, a team of ninth graders from HFA: Alameda School of Art and Design designed a carryall bag to meet the needs of the homeless. Their waterproof carryall has special features for surviving on the streets, such as separate pockets for clean and dirty laundry, a detachable pillow, and hidden pockets for storage. The learning and thinking process that led up to its design is typical of how design challenges unfold.

To kick off this learning experience, ninth graders toured a homeless shelter that's located near their school in San Antonio. Getting parents to agree to the site visit took some convincing. Students, too, had to confront their stereotypes. But interviewing volunteers and residents at the shelter helped them understand the practical concerns of people who have to transport their worldly goods wherever they go. They gained new understanding of the issues that cause homelessness, as well as the day-to-day challenges of surviving on the streets. This is the part of the design process that focuses on empathy—understanding the needs of the user.

After one student team's carryall design won top honors in an innovation contest hosted by the Smithsonian's Cooper-Hewitt, National Design Museum, Principal Jeffrey Flores explained the value of such learning experiences:

> Winning the competition gives our community, our families and our students a reassurance that there's a bigger picture when it comes to design. It's not just drawing or designing a video game—everything around us is involved in design. And our kids are realizing this, that it's more than just a backpack, and it's more than just making a backpack pretty. (Mianecki, 2011)

Prize money will go toward manufacturing a prototype of the design so that students can return to the shelter and present residents with a bag designed specifically for their use.

Connecting design challenges to academic standards takes planning. In the above example, ninth graders were also engaged in literature study, reading books like *The Things They Carried*. They applied their understanding of mathematics to compare volumes and estimate quantities of materials required to produce different designs. They used communication skills to interview users and make presentations about their designs. Throughout, they used teamwork skills to complete the assignment on time and within specific constraints.

Find an Opening

While HFLI has taken deliberate steps to integrate design thinking across the curriculum, other schools are finding their own ways to make an opening for this approach during the regular school day. Across the country as well as internationally, pockets of schools and individual teachers are introducing students to design thinking in electives, as part of traditional courses, through service learning, and in special events such as the World Meta Conference for young problem solvers that we heard about in chapter 1 (page 23).

In East Palo Alto, California, seventh and eighth graders have used design thinking to tackle problems ranging from combating bullying on campus to improving the quality of life for prisoners at a nearby facility where a student's father was incarcerated. In India, students used the same process to convince their municipal government to close street traffic to cars once a month so that children could use the space as a public playground and arts center (Barseghian, 2010).

The K–12 Lab uses a variety of approaches to introduce design thinking to formal and informal learning settings. Some teachers and school leaders come to the Stanford campus for summer "boot camps" that immerse them in the design process and help them build their toolkit of teaching strategies. Online resources also help tell success stories and disseminate effective implementation strategies.

Rich Crandall, who directs the K–12 Lab, says a key to successful implementation of design thinking is to build ownership from the ground up. "It's important that design thinking doesn't feel like an add-on or an extra thing that teachers have to do," he says. When teachers come to the idea willingly and see how it connects to what they are already doing in the classroom, they're more likely to invest the time and effort to learn new processes and strategies for working with students. A first step is often answering the question, "How are you going to get comfortable with this 'thing' that may at first seem foreign or extra?" For many teachers, the breakthrough comes when they recognize that design thinking doesn't compete with standards-based instruction but complements it, pushing students to higher-order thinking across the curriculum.

Effective leadership is "huge," Crandall adds. "It's vital for a principal to show trust. Teachers need to feel that someone has their back. It's a great combination to have a strong school leader who can give teachers the room to run with a good idea."

An idea like teaching empathy—central to the design process—may seem daunting at first. "But once we start to demystify it, teachers get it, and then they see how many things are possible," Crandall says. One practical step is simply to invite in a community member who has first-hand experience with the specific issue students are researching. "That person is an expert in this challenge," he explains. "There's a lot you can do, even with the constraints of school, to interact with people who have expertise." He's encouraged by the example of one teacher who struggled at first with an empathy exercise. "But then she went from not having any ideas to having so many ideas that she didn't know how to fit them all in. It was encouraging to see that flip."

The same thing happens when teachers start to brainstorm how to integrate design thinking into the curriculum. They may struggle at first, but then the ideas start to flow. In a language arts context, for instance, design thinking might mean interviewing a literary character (through role play) to understand point of view. In math or science, it might involve prototyping or modeling to test solutions. Collaborating with colleagues helps generate more ideas. "Once they start having these conversations, they start to see what's possible. Then it can be magic," Crandall adds.

One of the K–12 Lab's most ambitious professional development efforts is underway in Hawaii, where the entire state is embracing design thinking. Some 150 educators from thirty schools took part in a summer 2011 design thinking institute, sponsored by the Public Schools of Hawaii Foundation and facilitated by Crandall and colleagues. Messages from the governor and state superintendent of schools kicked off the workshop, sending the message that teachers have the go-ahead to engage in this challenging work. "They see this as a way to help move the state forward," Crandall explains. Industry leaders are also taking a strong interest in the initiative as a way to prepare students for careers that require creative thinkers. One principal came away from the workshop with a new idea for an ambitious design challenge to propose to his high school students: how might we design a program to embrace students who are losing interest in school and reengage them (Yamada, 2011)?

Design Thinking: How to Get Started

Like other expressions of project-based learning, design thinking requires a shift from traditional, teacher-driven instruction. That means teachers need to develop new strategies for working with students on open-ended questions for which there's not one right answer. They need to find opportunities to connect engaging design challenges to the standards-based curriculum. For design thinking to work well, teachers—and students—need time and support as they get comfortable in new roles as risk-takers and problem solvers, open to multiple solutions and perspectives.

Although brainstorming plays an important role at HFLI and at creative enterprises like IDEO, not everyone is a fan of the groupthink process. Citing research from management science and psychology, Jonah Lehrer writes in the *New Yorker*, "Brainstorming seems like an ideal technique, a feel-good way to boost productivity. But there is a problem with brainstorming. It doesn't work" (Lehrer, 2012). He notes that brainstorming results (measured by the number of creative ideas suggested) improve when participants take part in healthy debate and critique of each other's ideas. That's a departure from the HFLI rule to defer judgment while brainstorming. On the other hand, Lehrer has no doubts about the trend toward collaboration. Scientific journal articles and patents are increasingly likely to be credited to research teams rather than lone thinkers. Effective teams may not be brainstorming in the traditional sense, but they are finding ways to collaborate across disciplines. Before establishing class norms for brainstorming, then, teachers might want to engage their students in some action research. Try brainstorming sessions under different circumstances—deferring judgment first, then adding debate and critique—and see which conditions give rise to the most creative ideas.

Here are more suggestions to bring design thinking into your school setting:

- Learn to say, "Yes, and?" That's advice from Emily Pilloton, who uses this line often with her Studio H students. She explains, "Students would bring us a sketch or a model and we'd say, 'That's great. What else can you do?' *Yes, and?* is a way to foster creativity. Acknowledge that they've accomplished something, and then ask for something more."

- Start small to test this approach. Think about opportunities for introducing design challenges in electives, service learning, student clubs, and afterschool or summer programs.

- Consider what you would want to find out in a pilot project.

- Coordinate across disciplines to teach discrete skills. Art teachers, for example, can help students improve drawing skills for better sketch modeling. Media teachers can help students develop compelling presentations to share their design ideas publicly.

- Plan for how you might prepare to teach in this new way. For example, interested teachers might attend a design-thinking boot camp or observe a classroom design challenge in action. Colleagues might remodel an existing lesson plan or activity into a design challenge.

- Build a network of community members who can provide local expertise when it comes to understanding issues from the user's perspective.

- Apply this design-thinking strategy: build on others' ideas.

See appendix A (page 135) for more resources to bring design thinking to your classroom or learning community.

Strategy Spotlight: Think in Metaphors

At a glance: Innovators often borrow an idea from one context and introduce it to another. They're good at thinking in metaphors to generate new ideas.

When to use this strategy: To frame problems or generate possible solutions

Innovators make good use of metaphors. They often borrow an idea from one context and introduce it to another. Consider the StripeSpotter. Biologists working in Kenya used to joke among themselves that their painstaking work to identify individual zebras in the wild would be so much easier if they just had a barcode reader for wildlife. That would eliminate the need to capture and anesthetize zebras to implant tracking devices. The idea might have gone nowhere. But it turns out that a computer scientist from the University of Chicago happens to be married to an ecologist. Cross-disciplinary chats with her husband got Tanya Berger-Wolf thinking about looking at problems in ecology computationally, and her curiosity helped fuel development of an open-source system called StripeSpotter (Mullen, 2011).

When Berger-Wolf discussed the idea of a wildlife scanner with Princeton University evolutionary biologist Daniel Rubenstein, a world authority on zebras, he was quick to see the potential benefits. "We have always wanted a quickie way to let a computer do the identifying for us," Rubenstein told an interviewer (Mullen, 2011). Identification of individual animals in the wild has traditionally been a dangerous and time-consuming business. The game-changer, in this case, turned out to be the proliferation of cheap but high-quality digital cameras.

Instead of trapping and marking individual animals, field scientists could photograph them and build a dataset of images. The StripeSpotter algorithm analyzes these photos to produce the equivalent of a fingerprint for each zebra based on its unique stripe patterns. Now if researchers want to identify an animal, they can snap its photo and run it through StripeSpotter to search for a match. Photos are encoded with GPS information, enabling scientists to track locations and migration patterns (Lahiri, Tantipathananandh, Warungu, Rubenstein, & Berger-Wolf, 2011). It's easy to imagine how future innovations will bring StripeSpotter to mobile devices and open the way for more applications. The same technology may one day help researchers identify giraffes by their spots or elephants by the wrinkles in their trunks.

StripeSpotter was inspired by reimagining an existing technology (the barcode reader) to solve an entirely different need than the one for which it was designed. Sometimes, innovation unfolds when a process from one field is introduced to improve another.

The late Dr. Govindappa Venkataswamy was an Indian ophthalmologist who revolutionized eye care among the poor in his country. Dr. V, as he was widely known, had a breakthrough idea when he happened to visit a McDonald's restaurant. What if the extreme efficiency he saw in a fast-food chain could be introduced to cataract surgery? In India, at least twelve million people are blind. But 80 percent of these are cases that Dr. V recognized as "needless blindness," which could be prevented or successfully treated with surgery. The challenge wasn't to find a new cure but to design a faster, cheaper system for delivering cataract surgery to the elderly poor.

Aravind Eye Hospitals, which Dr. V founded as a retirement project, has grown to be one of the largest providers of eye care in the world. The Aravind model streamlines operating procedures so that one surgeon can perform as many as fifty surgeries a day. Aravind has continued to adopt more innovations that enable it to serve even more patients, especially those who can't afford to pay. For example, eye surgeons use replacement lenses that are produced at a fraction of the traditional cost. Aravind collaborated on their development. A sliding fee arrangement means that the poorest of the poor are able to receive care. Aravind's breakthrough ideas have spread far beyond India, helping to eradicate needless blindness around the world (Brilliant & Brilliant, 2007).

While Dr. V found inspiration in a fast-food joint, other innovators look to nature for ideas. This is the big idea behind biomimicry, which science writer Janine Benyus describes as innovation inspired by nature. After all, she points out, nature has been in the R&D business for billions of years. "After 3.8 billion years of research and development, failures are fossils, and what surrounds us is the secret to survival" (Benyus, 2002, p. 3).

One example is under development in the United Kingdom, where a software engineer is looking to the nematode worm for inspiration. As *New Scientist* explains:

> A giant robotic worm has slithered out of a 3D printer in the north of England—and one day its inventor hopes it could head for earthquake-hit cities in search of people trapped in collapsed buildings. Many engineers have tried to make robots that can worm their way into rubble, but few have taken a real worm for a model. Now Jordan Boyle at the University of Leeds, UK, has done just that: he has closely studied the nematode worm *Caenorhabditis elegans* and written control software that mimics its unique motion. (Marks, 2011)

Some innovators naturally think in metaphors at a young age. Aiden was a seventh grader when he took a hiking trip that started him on the road to discovery. While hiking in the Catskill Mountains in winter when the trees are bare of leaves, he noticed something surprising:

> I thought trees were a mess of tangled branches, but I saw a pattern in the way the tree branches grew. I took photos of the branches on different types of trees, and the pattern became clearer. The branches seemed to have a spiral pattern that reached up into the sky. I had a hunch that the trees had a secret to tell about this shape. (American Museum of Natural History, 2011)

Aiden discovered that the "secret formula in tree design" is none other than the Fibonacci sequence, a centuries-old numerical pattern that naturalists have identified in everything from the shape of the chambered Nautilus to the movement of galaxies.

Aiden didn't stop at that aha. His real innovation was to apply the same formula that helps trees collect sunlight for photosynthesis to the design of solar arrays. He reasoned that if solar collectors were built in a spiraling pattern, mimicking the sequence of tree branches, they would be more efficient at collecting light from the sun than flat panels. Aiden's breakthrough idea, which he prototyped and tested in his backyard, earned him a Young Naturalist Award from the American Museum of Natural History, along with a provisional patent.

Push Thinking to Extremes

While Aiden came up with his idea on his own, sometimes young innovators need encouragement to push their thinking. Extreme constraints offer one way to help spark ideas. In an episode of an HBO series *Masterclass*, renowned architect Frank Gehry coaches high school students to build a scale model of a new city. Time-lapse video shows students working frenetically to create what appears to be an elegant metropolis. Then Gehry bursts their bubble by pointing out that their design would only accommodate 70,000 or 80,000 people. "What if I told you it had to accommodate a million?" he asks with a grin. You can hear the groans from students who realize they have to rethink everything because of this extreme condition. He tells them, "Take it to where you can't stand it any longer" (Goodman & Simon, 2010).

Going to extremes creates artificial pressures that can produce gems of ideas. It's a strategy we can teach students to use to force new ways of looking at problems.

Hackathons, for instance, are competitive, short-term, but also intensely creative sprints for developers. Facebook holds them regularly to bring its engineers together around a shared challenge, and nonprofits use the same approach to "hack for good" around humanitarian issues. Turn time into an extreme challenge in the classroom to kick-start creativity and get ideas flowing.

In another take on extreme innovation, a popular interdisciplinary class at Stanford University challenges students to come up with extremely low-cost solutions to problems faced by the world's poorest citizens. Many of these problems have been solved in the Western world, but at a price that's out of reach in places like sub-Saharan Africa or rural India. By working with extreme funding constraints, students are designing breakthrough products. One team, for instance, set out to develop a low-cost baby warmer to save the lives of low-birth-weight infants in places where modern, electric incubators would be impractical. More newborns would survive with better access to incubators, but the $20,000 per unit cost, not to mention the need for electricity, makes this an impractical solution for rural villages. Students arrived at a solution that looks like a miniature sleeping bag. It features a removable insert that, when heated in hot water, maintains a steady temperature of 98 degrees Fahrenheit for up to four hours.

Give students opportunities to practice thinking at extremes by asking them to investigate issues of global importance or community concern. For example, in an interdisciplinary math and social studies project, students might start with statistical and geographic analyses to select an extreme challenge they want to explore. They might investigate:

- Which country (or demographic group) has the lowest life expectancy?

- What percentage of families in our school district are homeless?

- Which county in our state has the lowest literacy rate?

- Which segment of the population is the least likely to vote?

Students could tackle the challenge of designing their own solutions to these extreme challenges.

Borrow This Idea

Design thinking is useful for improving processes as well as products and can be a springboard for organizational change. As a staff, try using this approach to improve a school routine that's not working as well as it might.

For example, one school had a tradition of holding regular community meetings for students and staff. Over time, student attendance had dropped. Faculty used the design process to investigate the needs of users (such as students). Interviews with students revealed that they didn't like the morning meetings, because they were assigned to sit with their homerooms rather than their friends. Moreover, meetings happened mid-morning, a time when many students said they were hungry, and the agenda was driven by adults and held little interest for students. By engaging students on solutions, the school was able to introduce small changes, like allowing students to choose where to sit, offering snacks at the door, and having students plan and deliver programs. Attendance shot up and the experience became more valuable, for adults and students alike.

What routine needs improving at your school? How might you use design thinking to improve it?

Chapter 6

Making Room for Thinkers

How are schools making room for projects that encourage students to follow their interests and tackle authentic problems? Examples in this chapter suggest that schools are adjusting both physical spaces and schedules to make more room for thinkers.

When he was a junior in high school, a student named Michael developed a deep interest in infographics. His curiosity was piqued when he picked up his brother's copy of *Wired* magazine and his eye was drawn to intriguing, data-rich illustrations that he didn't yet have a name for. "I just knew I wanted to create something like them," he says.

I happened to meet Michael during a weekly webcast of *Teachers Teaching Teachers*. He joined the online conversation at the invitation of his teacher, Chris Sloan, from Judge Memorial Catholic High School in Salt Lake City, Utah.

As he continued discussing his interest in infographics, Michael made several key points that offered a window into his thinking process. For starters, he referenced Malcolm Gladwell's book *Outliers* as a source of inspiration. From reading Gladwell, Michael learned that people who develop expertise typically invest upward of ten thousand hours in pursuit of their passion. If Michael was going to get good at producing infographics—something he was intrinsically motivated to do—he knew he'd better get busy. So he challenged himself to create one new infographic a week. Michael also mentioned that he was born in 1992, the same year that the Internet launched. Growing up digital, he is used to having unfettered access to information. By exploring infographics, which present often complex information and data with elegantly simple graphics, he hoped to deepen his own thinking "about what that information means" (Allison, 2010).

Michael also understands how he can use technology to connect with a community. To get better at making infographics, he decided to make his learning public. So he set up a blog where he began publishing his infographics and inviting criticism. He posted not only his infographic creations but also thoughtful posts about how he had developed them. In words and pictures, he made his thinking visible.

Michael's exploration of infographics began as messing around, an activity that's common to innovators. At first, this intellectual exercise was disconnected from his life as a student. But Michael happened to be a student in Sloan's New Media class. Sloan, who also teaches English and is active in the National Writing Project, has expanded the curriculum to include writing and producing for a variety of media, from podcasting to video to—thanks to Michael—infographics. It's all about developing digital literacy as a 21st century skill.

Michael compares Sloan's class to the 20-percent time that Google gives its employees to noodle around with ideas. New Media offers Michael some mental breathing room within his heavily structured school day. But it's hardly idle time. The class inspires him to learn "inside and outside the classroom," he says, and allows him to connect his passions to his coursework. "Mr. Sloan's class enables us to explore to a point where we really want to learn. You can't find that in every class. I like being engaged," he says simply, and suggests that plenty of other students would welcome the same opportunity.

Sloan is wise enough to give students like Michael the freedom and space to take their learning as far as they choose to go. There are expectations and assignments, such as producing weekly podcasts. But there's also room for students to drive their own learning—and inspire their peers. "It's become a community of learners," Sloan says. "Students wind up teaching each other quite a bit" (Allison, 2010). Michael, for instance, might bring to class an interactive graphic that's caught his eye. That might trigger a class discussion about a news event, which some students will then elaborate on in a podcast.

Author Steve Johnson points out that the history of innovation is replete with stories of good ideas that occurred to people while they were out on a stroll (Johnson, 2010). Removed from the tasks of everyday life, you drift into a more associative state—the land of daydreams. He notes, "Given enough time, your mind will often stumble across some old connection that it had long overlooked, and you experience that delightful feeling of private serendipity: Why didn't I think of that before?" (Johnson, 2010, p. 110).

Some schools are managing to build more unstructured time into the school day. They're making room for thinkers.

Reframe School as an Innovation Workshop

Dennis Conner is a science teacher at St. Gregory School, a 6–12 independent school in Tucson, Arizona. His head of school, Jonathan Martin, is an outspoken advocate of reframing school so that students will have more opportunities to become thinkers, makers, and innovators. When Conner proposed a new elective class that would challenge students to design and build in a hands-on workshop environment, Martin was quick to approve.

The new course—called Technological Innovation: Design/Build—was inspired by Gever Tully's Tinkering School, grassroots innovation celebrations like Maker Faire, and publications and websites catering to the DIY crowd, such as *Instructables* and *MAKE Magazine*.

Offered for the first time during the 2010–2011 school year, the class immersed both students and teachers in an unfamiliar learning environment. Instead of giving specific assignments, Conner challenged students to come up with proposals for things they wanted to try to build or invent. The word *try* is deliberate. "Plenty of these attempts won't work, especially on the first try," Conner acknowledges one spring afternoon, as he kept an eye on students at work in a large, open space outfitted with a variety of hand tools, electronics, welding equipment, and inexpensive materials like old bike parts and lengths of lumber.

At the back of the workshop, doors open to a patch of asphalt on the edge of playing fields, giving students more room to spread out on big projects. It's also a place where learning—and struggling—happens in plain sight. "Some students will take on an ambitious idea, but then they'll be ready to give up when they hit a snag," Conner observes. Seeing other students persist, even when it's tough, provides positive peer pressure to keep at it. "That can be enough to help them get over hurdles."

Alex's giant trike project is a good example. He challenged himself to build an oversized bicycle as a "crazy experiment." He considered the idea doable, given his understanding of mechanics and the ready availability of spare bike parts. But when he tried to expand the scale of a two-wheeler, he encountered unexpected hurdles that had to do with balance, alignment, gearing systems, and more. That led to plan B: design and build a really large tricycle. Conner gave the student leeway to experiment and adapt his thinking instead of rushing in with suggestions. Once he welded the frame and got the wheels and gears assembled, Alex ran into even more issues involving steering. Each new problem challenged him to be flexible, to adapt, and to keep redesigning. His reflection at the end: "I got to be way more creative in this class than any other classes. And we wound up with a pretty quality trike" (Martin, 2011).

Another student named Becca decided to try to build a *theremin*, an electronic musical instrument that uses magnetic energy to produce eerie sounds. Invented by a Russian physicist nearly a century ago, the instrument is making a comeback on the avant-garde music scene. A musician plays it without ever touching the instrument. Instead, performance involves deliberate hand-waving between two antennae. Becca's motivation was simple: "They look cool. I wanted to see if I could make one."

She began with a mail-order kit, but it came with poorly written instructions and a mess of unlabeled parts. "It took a lot of troubleshooting—three weeks to solve one problem," Becca says. Meanwhile, she was learning about everything from the physics of sound to soldering. "I kept modifying it. Whenever I felt about ready to give up, I'd envision having it done. I kept thinking, 'It will be great when it's working.'" Eventually, she got there.

Although Becca worked primarily on her own on the theremin project, she has tackled other projects with teams. "I found out that I love working with a group. I like being the leader. I'm able to get others to focus." She also enjoys the atmosphere of the workshop space—purposeful but relaxed at the same time. "It's completely different from my other classes. It's less structured, and I like that. It feels like a break in my day. It kind of calms me down compared to AP history or math. You have more freedom and choice, but you also have to motivate yourself. Not giving up is a big thing I learned."

Another team of students decided to build something to create more shade on their desert campus. "We wanted a new place to hang out," one boy explains. They decided it would be even better if they could recharge their netbooks at the same time. Their solution: a ramada with a solar-powered charging station.

Once they had the idea in mind, they dug into research. They discovered that their shelter would require components like solar panels, inverters, and other elements that couldn't be built out of spare parts in the workshop. They also needed building permits. Using Google

SketchUp, they prepared a design plan that made their thinking visible and became part of their formal proposal to the head of school. Once he authorized a small construction budget, they were on their way. By late spring—a few months after inspiration first struck—the ramada was ready for use.

These students found satisfaction in building something tangible that benefits everyone on campus. What's more, as one student says, "It's a chance to do what I want to do instead of the teacher's agenda. Coming up with our own project was exciting." Another says he was surprised by how much freedom the class offered. "The teacher says, 'Do what you want, and I'll help you.' We have so much autonomy, but we learned about science, technology, electronics."

They also developed a deeper understanding of what innovation is all about and how it's now part of their lives. "It's thinking in a new way to find solutions," one student begins, and soon his teammates pile on and finish one another's thoughts: "Once you start exploring ideas, it kind of sets off a chain reaction. . . . You start asking, what can I do with this? Being in a team definitely helps speed up the thinking process. Ideas come faster. . . . We had a lot of discussions and looked at things from different angles."

From the teacher's perspective, it takes trial and error to figure out the best way to scaffold student learning with such open-ended projects. "I try to stay in the background but offer suggestions when I see them struggling," Conner says. Watching Alex make his big trike, for instance, was like watching "a cascade of problems. He changed the thickness of the frame, and that led to a big new problem: the chain wouldn't run. Each step required more problem solving."

Many of these first-generation projects lean toward the whimsical, but that doesn't limit the opportunities for serious learning. At least one student, Derek, has used the elective to go deeper into the field where he hopes to focus his career.

Derek challenged himself to make an iPhone app for his school. A self-directed learner, he has surpassed his teachers in his understanding of coding. He's also an adept videographer. To learn what he needs to know about computer science or digital technology, he listens to lectures at iTunes U and finds other online resources. "Designing an app, you have to think about what makes your idea different. What sets it apart? I'm exploring original ideas, higher quality, doing something that no one's done before. I'm excited to see where it goes. This is preparing me for what I want to do for the rest of my life."

Thinking Space: How to Get Started

Derek's comment echoes a sentiment I've heard from students in a variety of settings, both public and private, where they have room to explore interests in depth and challenge themselves on difficult projects. Making space for thinkers, like so many other innovation strategies, can start with small steps—whether that means physical space or space in the schedule.

Here are steps to consider:

- **Start with an elective**—That's how Conner launched his design/build workshop. An elective that emphasizes open-ended projects offers a forum for testing student interest, evaluating results, and exploring connections to content areas.

- **Offer 20-percent time**—Some teachers are adopting Google's strategy by scheduling 20 percent of class time for open-ended student work. (See more examples in the following sections.) Before giving this approach a test run, think about the scaffolding students may need to make effective use of unstructured time. Use journals, project logs, informal check-ins, and other formative assessments to encourage students to reflect on what they're learning and why it matters. Set expectations, such as having students share the results of their 20-percent projects.

- **Go schoolwide**—Consider an innovation project that challenges students across grade levels and subject areas. (Remember how the Dots in Blue Water project eventually engaged every student?) Schoolwide projects spark teacher collaboration and help to establish a culture that says, "We're all thinkers here."

Strategy Spotlight: Take Time to Mess Around

At a glance: A playful, risk-free, "messing around" atmosphere can be conducive to generating good ideas.

When to use this strategy: During problem identification, idea generation, or when refining ideas

Unlocking the mysteries of the universe is serious business, yet physicists Andre Geim and Konstantin Novoselov make room for play in the lab at the University of Manchester in England. Geim reserves Friday nights for exploring particularly zany ideas, such as messing around with sticky tape and pencils. That's what these scientists were doing when they stumbled on *graphene*, a one-atom-thick layer of carbon that has the structure of chicken wire. It may soon revolutionize electronics. Their discovery earned them the Nobel Prize in Physics in 2010.

With his Friday-night experiments, Geim has created a serendipitous climate, which makes room for creativity, coincidence, and playfulness. Geim describes his unconventional process this way: "The only thing I can do is enlarge the small chance that I stumble on something valuable" (Institute of Brilliant Failure, 2011). When the Nobel Prize was announced, Mark Miodownik from King's College London, told the *Telegraph* that the award "will bring a smile to the face of every scientist because it shows you can still get a Nobel Prize by mucking about in a lab" (Alleyne, 2010).

I've heard similar praise for "mucking about" at highly competitive student science fairs, such as the Intel International Science and Engineering Fair, where an annual highlight is the panel discussion among Nobel laureates. Prompted by students' questions, these elite physicists, biologists, and chemists reminisce about their own youthful forays into scientific investigation. They tend to wax nostalgic when talking about basement workshops where they took stuff apart and tinkered with their first inventions. I've also heard them voice concern about the limited opportunities many of today's students have to mess around with stuff. You can't take the case off a digital device, for instance, and easily figure out how it works; circuit boards don't give up their secrets the way that old-fashioned toasters do. Yet, messing around continues to be an important strategy for innovators.

Remember Jeff Sturges, who created the Mt. Elliott Makerspace to give Detroit youth a community workshop for informal learning? His ideas for the Makerspace were shaped in part by reading up on the habits of innovators. As he explains, "When you study the great innovators, you find out that most of them had access to tools and workshops. They were given time to play around with things. They got encouragement from their peers. They also did a lot of problem solving based on need."

Allowing time to mess around with ideas can be especially useful at what experts call the "fuzzy front end." This is the early stage in idea development when the task is to clarify which problem you're trying to solve and why it matters. It's also a good time to consider, Why hasn't anyone else solved this yet? Where's the gap that I might be able to fill (Product Arts, n.d.)?

Let's consider two examples that show how messing around can lead to positive change: creating physical space and creating space in the schedule for innovation.

Create Physical Space

At Monticello High in Charlottesville, Virginia, students were busy at work in a room stuffed with digital recording gear. Located in a back corner of the media center, the small space had recently been cleared of storage boxes and converted to a digital media lab with the enthusiastic endorsement of veteran librarian Joan Ackroyd. Shortly before arriving at this school, she had attended a conference that gave her fresh ideas about reinventing the school library to be a more active learning space. "I'm passionate about students using technology to communicate their thoughts and connect with others," she says.

She found a kindred spirit in her colleague David Glover, an instructional media specialist who also teaches English. Glover is young enough to consider himself a millennial. Long interested in music, he hasn't forgotten his own high school experience. "I always wished there was a place to go in the building where I could meet other students who were into music, too," he says. As a teen, he spent his free hours at a community center equipped for making music, but that meant his passion was separate from his school day. What if the media center could blur those boundaries, giving kids a place in school to connect around their interests?

The timing was good for trying out a new idea. Across the district, other librarians were also looking for ways to reimagine the school library, which was one of several innovation initiatives headed by district administrator Becky Fisher that have opened new opportunities to experiment and hold collegial discussions. Fisher discovered that change can begin with a small step, such as removing the long library tables that are better suited to adult meeting needs than kids' active learning. She's seen some schools change the library's atmosphere by replacing traditional furniture with beanbag chairs that encourage leisure reading. Others are adding stations equipped for different kinds of media use, such as audio stations for listening to podcasts or for making recordings. Each time the library team meets, Fisher challenges her colleagues to "go back to your school and try one new thing."

Glover's first step was just talking with students: "I asked them what would be cool." Many students were enthusiastic about the idea of a place to hang out and produce their own digital music or edit videos. He enlisted interested students to help him clear out boxes and set up used equipment. Then he and Ackroyd sat back and watched to see what would happen.

Early in the school year, new students typically do a walk-through orientation session in the library. Ackroyd decided to make the exercise more interactive by giving students Flip cameras and asking them to make short videos about how they might use eight learning stations in the library. The new room was one of them. "We invited students to tell us what they thought this space should be," recalls Ackroyd. "We started with a blank canvas."

Once students realized they could use the room however they wanted, they began showing up during their free time. First ten, then twenty, and before long, more than forty students a day were making active use of the new space. There's just one catch, Glover explains, "They have to have a purpose to be here. Some students will come in and just listen at first, and that's fine. Then one day, we'll see them sit down at the computer and try to use some software to write a song. They might get frustrated. Maybe another month goes by. But at some point, they get locked into the idea, *I'm going to do this*. You can see them become determined to learn. They start learning from their peers who are farther along, figuring out what it takes to build a project."

The best moments happen when "we see students get inspired, and then take their idea and translate it into something real."

Along with learning to use unfamiliar digital tools to record their creativity, students are also undergoing internal changes. "It's like rewiring," Glover says. "They start to feel the motivation." Students who are used to following instructions may struggle at first with self-directed learning. "They don't know what they're supposed to be doing when it's all up to them," he says, but they soon figure it out.

What's happening in this little room at Monticello High has caught Fisher's attention. An innovator at heart, she keeps her radar up for good ideas that can spread. She's been impressed by the positive social interactions that unfold here, often among students who otherwise would have no reason to interact. Coming together around shared, creative interests, they're naturally inclined to help each other. One student, for instance, has found his passion for recording original beats that others use as the backbone for new songs. "Kids are mixing by race, gender, socioeconomics. They want to be there," Fisher says. "The only problem they've had is that some would rather skip class—and go to the library!" That has her pondering new questions about blurring the edges of learning spaces. "How can we infuse that excitement into the rest of school, so that it's the place where kids would rather be? How can we see the library spill into the school and the school spill into the library?"

"I never dreamed how this little space would affect students," adds Ackroyd. "Students tell us it brings meaning to their day. Projects they do in here set a new standard for work in their regular classes." One student, for instance, dropped in before school to play a song he had just recorded. Nine more students gathered around, offering admiring reviews. The boy's face lit up as he said, "That's my motivation for the day."

In this unstructured space, students naturally offer their peers critical feedback or friendly encouragement. "There's a real spirit of cooperation in here. It's a community," Ackroyd says. At the same time, Glover recognizes a healthy spirit of competition that challenges students to be more original, more creative. "If somebody puts out a new song, you hear everyone else saying, 'I've got to make a song now.' I'm looking to bring that same ownership into my regular classroom. It's powerful."

Create Schedule Space

Before regular classes kick into gear at Crozet Elementary in Crozet, Virginia, veteran teacher Paula White welcomes a mixed-age group to her classroom for some high-interest activities that involve investigating math concepts. Elsewhere around the school, small groups of students are huddling for activities that have to do with architecture, computer programming in Scratch, digital moviemaking, and a host of other topics. Parents arrive to contribute their expertise, along with other community members who are knowledgeable enough about particular topics to volunteer as mentors. Welcome to Mastery Extension, a scheduling innovation designed to help students discover their passions.

The school previously used a pull-out approach to serve students with special needs, ranging from gifted education to remediation. Mastery Extension changes the game by giving all students a daily opportunity to expand their interests and enjoy more voice and choice about learning. The small groups also allow students who need support in specific areas to get more focused attention without being pulled out of the regular school day. Although some students still need remediation, both teachers and students are finding new opportunities during this morning time to "work on their weaknesses through their strengths," as White puts it.

White, a gifted resource teacher, says the experience is causing students to see teachers in a new way as the old lines between school and community start to blur. "This is causing them to think about, Who has knowledge to share? Who can help them develop their ideas?" she says. At the same time, she adds, "Teachers are seeing strengths and interests emerge that they might not have recognized before in students." Teachers are also getting opportunities to emerge from their own classrooms and see their colleagues in action. Of course, as White notes, this means that teachers "have to be open to new things."

In many systems, the school schedule is untouchable. But for schools that are willing to try new approaches, time can be an interesting variable to play with. At Science Leadership Academy, for instance, class schedules rotate regularly so that students don't associate a particular subject with a certain time of day. Otherwise, a "morning person" may wind up disliking math just because it comes at the day's end. It takes a little more effort to rotate the schedule, but it's the kind of small but powerful shift that this school embraces because it's better for students.

When White wrote about the Mastery Extension idea on the Cooperative Catalyst blog, teachers from across the country chimed in with comments about how they are shifting schedules to create more open-ended learning opportunities. For instance, a high school science teacher has declared Fridays "Google Time," when students have 20 percent of the week to research scientific topics that interest them (with the expectation that they will share their findings with classmates). Another teacher described a "push for change" at her school that started by asking students two questions: (1) What do you want to be when you grow up? and (2) What do you do outside of school hours that you love? She continued, "Then we started seeking out ways to have that be school. If we are smarter about the time we spend together, we shouldn't be waiting till 3, or summer, or after we graduate to do the things we love" (White, 2010).

Borrow This Idea

Nueva School, an independent prek–8 school for the gifted in Hillsborough, California, has built a 3,500-square-foot "innovation lab" designed in collaboration with students, Nueva staff, and professors from the Stanford d.school. It includes a woodshop and big bays where students can build and refine prototypes. Since making the space available, the school has started to see a change in how students use their time—changing the culture of the school to a place for makers.

> Similar to Google's "20 Percent Time" initiative, the I-Lab's Monday lunches allow students to pursue more self-directed inquiry. On the first day of every week, the I-Lab is open during lunch for students to work on their own projects. The first dedicated participants were 2nd and 4th graders, who used the time to build prototypes as varied as doll houses and dental instruments.

> As the I-Lab continues to evolve, students have begun to use the space to fit their needs and learning goals. For example, students are beginning to independently initiate group brainstorms in the I-Lab space. This indicates that students have begun to internalize the message that design thinking involves more than building prototypes! (d.school, n.d.a)

Similarly, YouMedia is a national initiative to remake libraries into informal digital learning spaces for teens. The concept was prototyped at the Chicago Public Library as a follow-up to the John D. and Catherine T. MacArthur Foundation's landmark research project on how youth engage with digital media. Chicago's YouMedia center is a place for teens to use digital tools to be makers and creators of content. It offers them time and opportunities to hang out with peers in a media-rich space, mess around to explore new interests and discover new tools with help from mentors, and geek out to take learning deeper through workshops and independent study. Now, the MacArthur Foundation is teaming up with the Institute of Museum and Library Services to take this concept to thirty more sites.

As lessons learned from this national innovation effort are being documented and shared, a picture is emerging of what this kind of informal learning looks like. These are spaces in which learning is youth centered, interest driven, reflective, about making and doing, collaborative, nimble and flexible, and cross-disciplinary. Adults provide mentoring and are supported with professional development. Community partners lend more expertise (Ito et al., 2010; Jenkins, 2006).

By making space in the regular school day, how might you bring more of these characteristics to your school setting? As an action step, focus on one thing you might do or suggest now—with space, time, or another variable of the school equation—to create more room for thinkers.

Chapter 7

Taking Advantage of Technology

Innovators are good at looking ahead, imagining potential benefits that others can't yet see. New technologies have the potential to be game-changers if they can open new opportunities for learning. This chapter shows how introducing students to engineering—especially with an emerging technology such as the tabletop digital fabricator—is happening in elementary classrooms through a process that emphasizes key innovation strategies.

Digital fabricators are becoming small enough to fit on a desktop, cheap enough for widespread distribution, and powerful enough to transform product design, manufacturing, and—just maybe—education. What are they? Just as a laser printer follows your computer's commands to print documents, fabricators follow digital commands to produce three-dimensional objects. Press a button and bingo, the fab "prints" you a 3-D widget, gear, coffee cup, or whatever you have programmed it to fabricate by putting down layers of wax, plastic, or other material—even Play-Doh.

Digital fabricators offer a fast-track way to take a raw idea from the mind's eye to real life. Being able to represent thinking is important at any age, but it is especially so for children who are exploring new concepts. "Young students typically have not had the opportunity to see their concepts make the trip from an initial conceptual idea to a final physical form," explains education professor Glen Bull. "The advent of personal fabrication can allow students this opportunity for the first time" (Bull & Groves, 2009, p. 36).

Digital fabricators aren't new. For years, they have been used to produce prototypes by those with the resources to invest in high-end manufacturing equipment. What's new is the low-cost version. A kit currently in the works is expected to bring the cost of a 3-D fabricator to about $1,000. That's an affordable enough price point so that these devices can start showing up everywhere from the home desktop to the community workshop to the classroom. And that has some big thinkers excited.

Neil Gershenfeld from MIT's Center for Bits and Atoms started to recognize the potential several years ago when he offered a class called "How to Make (Almost) Anything." This wildly popular class turned students loose with laser cutters, programmable 2-D and 3-D printers, and assorted materials. Students who were steeped in theoretical classes seized the opportunity to make real stuff in what MIT called a Fab Lab. Their products were highly individualized, tailored to what Gershenfeld calls "a market of one person."

Before long, MIT started sending portable Fab Labs, equipped with about $20,000 worth of tools, to inner-city Boston, the Bronx, and impoverished villages around the world. In each outreach location, Gershenfeld and his colleagues noticed a similar progression. First came empowerment—the sheer joy of discovery as adults and children began making things for themselves. From there, the work quickly progressed to serious problem solving of issues relating to energy, conservation, agriculture, and business. "Real invention is happening in these labs," Gershenfeld explains in a TED talk about the initiative. Community members are teaching each other to use the tools to design and produce solutions to local problems. It's all about learning at the edge. As Gershenfeld puts it, "This is the kind of tool that breaks everybody's boundaries" (Gershenfeld, 2006).

Grow Opportunities

It didn't take long for the Fab Lab concept to capture the imagination of Glen Bull, who we met in chapter 2. An educational technology pioneer from the Curry Center for Education at the University of Virginia, Bull has an eye for emerging tools that have the potential to transform K–12 education. Bull's energy is now focused on introducing engineering concepts in the elementary grades, with digital fabricators playing a supporting role in instruction. He anticipates a game-changer with an emerging concept called Fab@School. "It's kind of the future," he says simply. Bull is leading the Fab@School research initiative together with Robert Berry, elementary education professor at University of Virginia. The multiyear project, funded by a National Science Foundation Innovative Technologies Grant, includes additional partners from both private and nonprofit organizations along with other universities and several school districts.

The big goal of Fab@School is to improve math and science education and address the United States' much-discussed STEM crisis. If students can gain a better understanding of math and science concepts in the elementary years, then they will arrive at high school and college ready for a deeper dive into engineering, computer science, and other STEM fields.

Bull has brainstormed with his University of Virginia engineering colleagues about the backward planning that's needed to prepare more students for the STEM career track. For example, he asks, "What should students know and be able to do when they come into the School of Engineering?" He has also talked with K–12 teachers about what this means going all the way back to elementary school. Part of the challenge he sees is simply making math and science education more enjoyable, so that students are inclined to stick with these fields. His own delight is obvious when he sees someone get excited about math and science, whether it's an elementary student who suddenly has her heart set on becoming an engineer or a graduate student who has just learned how to amplify sound. "You need to do things that show you math and science are useful," he insists.

Using Fab@School equipment and instructional approaches that introduce engineering concepts, elementary students design and make objects that show their solutions to specific challenges. They might start by drawing a simple geometric object, like a cube, on a computer screen. They can rotate it on screen, adjust the size and color, and view it from any angle. When they're ready to proceed, modeling software turns the drawing into a "net" (such as an unfolded cube), which is then produced on paper or cardstock using a special printer that scores, perforates, and cuts the net. Students use this printed material, along with low-tech scissors and glue, to build their 3-D model. If it doesn't come together as planned, that opens an opportunity for them to talk through their thinking and, perhaps, reveal misconceptions. Then they can adjust their design and try again.

Modeling projects can go from simple to complex. In a social studies and math project about communities, for instance, students might design and build to scale a model city made up of skyscrapers and connecting bridges. Teachers can set up challenges to include specific constraints that students have to meet en route to their solution. That enables teachers to emphasize key concepts, such as calculating angles or rotational symmetry.

Elementary teacher Paula White is among the K–12 educators piloting Fab@School at Crozet Elementary in Virginia. "Engineering
design is really a process for solving problems and a language to explain
thinking," she says. "It fits naturally into what I do with kids all the
time." One engineering challenge, for instance, involved measurement,
comparing ratios, "all kinds of concepts students never realized they
were studying. It was fun for them. They were constantly trying out
stuff." For another project, students teamed up to design and build a
miniature carnival fun house complete with LED lights and mirrors.

In another classroom in the same school, fourth graders designed
and built a model skate park. This high-interest project required them
to understand and apply math concepts, such as symmetry, angles,
and proportion, along with the concepts of force, motion, and energy.
Meanwhile, the engineering process gave their teacher, Tammy Scot,
opportunities to observe, ask questions, and draw out students' thinking. Simple questions—Why doesn't that work? What changes do you
need to make? Why do you think that will work better?—prompted
students to reflect aloud, providing formative assessment that enabled
their teacher to address any misconceptions (Bell, 2011).

Open-ended engineering challenges "have choice built in. There's
not one right answer," White says. "That means students aren't playing
the game of 'the teacher asks the question and I feed her the answer she
wants.' Kids who are thinkers," she adds, "especially appreciate that."

The evolution of Fab@School is worth watching, and Bull and his
team of energetic graduate students are using the process of innovation to fine-tune and expand this initiative. Parallel efforts are underway to develop hardware (with an engineering team led by Hod Lipson
at Cornell) and software (led by Peggy Healy Stearns for FableVision).
Fab@School efforts also have received support from the MacArthur
Foundation's Digital Media and Learning Competition.

Meanwhile, elementary teachers at partner schools in Virginia,
Hawaii, Georgia, and abroad are paired up with the research team to
test and fine-tune instructional strategies in the classroom. These field
efforts are also informing the professional development approaches that
will enable Fab@School to take hold and achieve large-scale results.

The goal is not just getting fabrication equipment into a handful of
schools, but setting the stage for sustained efforts at problem solving,
critical thinking, and deep understanding of important STEM concepts. To help the initiative expand, good ideas for the classroom are

being shared on an open-source platform and documented in YouTube videos and reflective blogs. For instance, www.maketolearn.org is an online resource about digital fabrication in education, which is a project of the Society for Information Technology & Teacher Education.

Over the years, a key lesson Bull has learned about introducing new ideas to education is that it's critical to get off to a good start. That's why Fab@School is being piloted under hothouse conditions—just right for innovation to take hold. Before the idea can go to scale, he knows it's critical to invest time first in testing, refining, and iterating through user feedback. To encourage and sustain innovation in education, wild ideas and new technologies aren't enough. Patience and practicality are also required.

Engineering: How to Get Started

Although teaching engineering in K–12 is an idea that's still relatively young, a report by the National Academy of Engineering and the National Research Council (Katehi, Pearson, & Feder, 2009) identified general principles to inform program design. These principles suggest good starting points for introducing children's engineering.

1. Teach students the design process, which is highly iterative, open ended (a problem may have many possible solutions), and offers a meaningful context for learning scientific, mathematical, and technological concepts.

2. Incorporate important and developmentally appropriate mathematics, science, and technology knowledge and skills, including scientific inquiry, math modeling, and computational thinking. Technology can be useful for activities such as testing and measurement, data analysis, and visualization.

3. Foster engineering "habits of mind," which include systems thinking, creativity, optimism, collaboration, communication, and attention to ethical considerations. (Katehi et al., 2009, pp. 150–152)

A practical way to apply these suggestions is to use design briefs as part of instruction. Design briefs are commonly used in the engineering and design fields to frame a problem and identify any constraints that may limit solutions. Children's Engineering Educators, an organization of elementary educators, suggests incorporating these five elements in design briefs for K–5 students: (1) background statement to provide content, (2) challenge statement to define the problem, (3) criteria by which solutions will be assessed, (4) available materials, and (5) available tools.

Design briefs are not limited to engineering projects. In the middle school science classroom, for example, a design brief can set the stage for active learning through inquiry. In "Inquiry by Design Briefs," the authors suggest framing a science project with a context statement (for instance, define a scientific concept), a scenario (short vignette to set the stage), a challenge (specific problem to be solved), and limitations and rules (Gooding & Metz, 2007). This open-ended instructional approach "places added responsibility onto the shoulders of the learners and describes what is required but not how to get there" (Gooding & Metz, 2007, p. 35).

Strategy Spotlight: Learn to Fail

At a glance: Learn from failed attempts by paying attention to what didn't work and why.

When to use this strategy: When refining ideas, during prototyping, when reflecting on results

When ninth graders walk into Matt Van Kouwenberg's classroom at Science Leadership Academy in Philadelphia, they don't know quite what to expect. The course title is Engineering, a discipline that students here explore deeply throughout their high school experience. They might have a general idea of what happens in this field, especially if they happen to know some professional engineers. Yet few students arrive with a deep understanding of the processes that engineers use to generate ideas and refine solutions. That's why Van Kouwenberg starts them off with a hands-on experience.

After an ice-breaker activity on the first day of class, he launches into a problem for students to solve. "You're going to build a wind turbine out of office supplies," the teacher explains. They talk briefly about definitions so that students understand the basic concept of what a wind turbine does. Other than that, their charge is clear: go figure it out for yourselves. Before turning them loose, Van Kouwenberg asks students not to rush to Google to search for someone else's ideas.

As the teacher busies himself in the classroom, he watches to see what students do next. Some just sit, looking puzzled. These are the ones who are used to the teacher giving them the answer if they wait quietly long enough. But a few are up and moving around the room in search of materials. When they find a drawer plainly labeled "office supplies," they dig in—pausing just long enough to get a quick nod of permission from the teacher. Van Kouwenberg is pleased when one student asks, "Can we use a power drill?" That's an opportunity to offer a just-in-time safety lesson and also remind students that it's OK to use tools to accomplish a task.

There's a lot going on in this scenario, but the key message comes across during the first debriefing. After letting students struggle with their wind turbine design for a class period, Van Kouwenberg demonstrates the rather poor model he made. A gentle breeze from a fan is enough to knock it over. That's his opening to ask students, "What do you notice? What could I modify? What's going on here?" He makes one design modification on the spot, tests it again—and discovers that it's even worse than the previous version. Then students get a chance to rework their own designs, internalizing the message that problem solving is an iterative process.

"The whole idea here is that the first or second design is not going to work. It may take them two or three or five iterations before they get it to work. Every project will be different, but I want them to fail fast and fail often," he explains.

This is a new message to students who have come to equate "failure" with the dreaded "F" grade. In this class, projects are graded on effort and process, not on getting the right answer. Indeed, there isn't one right answer to the problems that students tackle in engineering. "If you're engaged with the project, even if it's not close to working, it's still 'A' work. This is about the process," he tells them. Solutions get better through brainstorming, testing, reflecting, analyzing, documenting what you notice, and making modifications. "It's about multiple iterations, getting comfortable with failure. That's not a bad word in this class," he keeps telling students, who often need some convincing. "Just don't fail the same way twice."

When students grow into their new role as idea-generators, wonderful things start to happen. A year after their introduction to engineering, a team of tenth graders from Science Leadership Academy went on to design a device that uses readily available materials to turn food waste into biodiesel fuel. Another team figured out how to purify water using a parabolic design made of cardboard, bits of broken mirrors, and a tiny solar panel. Through connections to the world beyond the classroom, both ideas are now making their way to the developing world, where such frugal innovations have the potential to improve lives.

Learning from failure is a mantra of thinkers who use an iterative process to test ideas, keep what works, and discard what doesn't. On a wall inside Facebook headquarters, for instance, is a poster that reads "Move fast. Break stuff." It's a strategy commonly used in fields ranging from engineering and design to science research to social innovation. Take apart polished ideas, and you'll often see that they took dramatic turns between inspiration and implementation.

The Apple Newton was a colossal flop back in the 1990s. Even *Doonesbury* comic creator Garry Trudeau ridiculed the handwriting recognition software that was supposed to be a key feature of the new personal digital assistant. At more than $1,000, the Newton was expensive. Marketing campaigns asked the intriguing question, "What is Newton?" but didn't make the case for why anyone would want one. Soon after Steve Jobs returned to Apple in 1997, the Newton was scrapped. When the iPad launched in 2010 however, technophiles couldn't help but follow the bread crumbs back to Apple's original tablet device. But this time around, the software wasn't buggy. Marketing campaigns built so much buzz that people lined up outside Apple stores the night before the iPad went on sale. Apple didn't give up on personal devices after its first failed attempt but instead figured out how to make them better.

Such successes often emerge only after repeat attempts and hard-won lessons. Harvard Business School Professor Amy Edmondson calls the wisdom of learning from failure "incontrovertible" (Edmondson, 2011). Yet the lessons of failure are exceedingly difficult to capture, she acknowledges. In an issue of *Harvard Business Review* devoted to failure, she writes:

> The attitudes and activities required to effectively detect and analyze failures are in short supply in most companies, and the need for context-specific learning strategies is underappreciated. Organizations need new and better ways to go beyond lessons that are superficial ("Procedures weren't followed") or self-serving ("The market just wasn't ready for our great new product"). That means jettisoning old cultural beliefs and stereotypical notions of success and embracing

failure's lessons. Leaders can begin by understanding how
the blame game gets in the way. (Edmondson, 2011)

What might it take to build a culture where failure is not only toler-
ated but celebrated?

Engineers Without Borders (EWB) has set out to turn failure into
a source of rich learning. EWB recently launched a website called
Admitting Failure (www.admittingfailure.com), where "good failures"
are showcased and used as springboards for serious reflection. The
motto—"Failure's only bad when it's repeated"—echoes the advice Van
Kouwenberg gives his students. On the website, EWB discusses its
own missteps about development projects in Africa and encourages
other organizations to deconstruct what hasn't worked and why. The
goal is a more open, transparent conversation that will benefit everyone
attempting to do the hard work of international development.

A similar message is shared at FailFaire events, where people publicly—and, often, with good humor—recount efforts at global problem
solving that didn't work as intended. The first such event was organized by MobileActive, an organization that promotes mobile technology development for social good. As the FailFaire blog explains, "We
believe that only if we understand what doesn't work in this field, and
stop pushing our failures under the rug, can we collectively learn and
get better, more effective, and have greater impact as we go forward"
(Heatwole, 2010). To encourage others to learn from failure, organizers of FailFaire have shared their approach for hosting such an event.
Their open-source protocols include (Heatwole, 2010):

- **Get the right people in the room**—People who are there to
  learn.

- **Plan presentations so that presenters address key
  points**—What was the project? What were you trying to do?
  Where did it go wrong? What would you do differently next
  time? What lessons can be learned?

- **Set the right tone**—Be nonjudgmental; balance levity with
  responsibility; make it about learning, not blaming.

Bring the FailFaire atmosphere to professional development by creating opportunities to discuss classroom activities or projects that didn't
work as planned. Using the protocols developed by FailFaire organizers will help keep the emphasis on learning rather than placing blame.

As a driving question for this professional learning project, consider asking: what can we learn from less-than-successful efforts?

Borrow This Idea

The Marshmallow Challenge started in the business world but is quickly migrating to the classroom—and for good reason. It's a low-tech, low-risk team-building activity that demonstrates the value of learning from failure and improving through iteration. The rules, shared in a popular TED talk by Tom Wujec and his accompanying website (http://marshmallowchallenge.com), are deceptively simple: using twenty sticks of dry spaghetti, a yard of tape, and a yard of string, build the tallest freestanding structure you can that will support the weight of one marshmallow. Work in teams of four. You have eighteen minutes. Go!

Physics teacher Frank Noschese explains why the Marshmallow Challenge belongs in his classroom—and any classrooms where failure is a step toward learning:

> You see, the unsuccessful teams typically wait until the 18 minutes are over before putting the marshmallow on top. In contrast, the teams that successfully build a tower which can support the marshmallow typically go through several cycles of building and testing during the 18 minutes. Build, test, modify, retest, repeat. It's a feedback loop . . . In the Marshmallow Challenge, the successful spaghetti towers would not be possible without continuous testing and failing. That is why success and failure must be celebrated with equal enthusiasm and that as teachers we must encourage continuous risk-taking. (Noschese, 2011)

Repeat the Marshmallow Challenge after students gain more experience working in teams and using an iterative approach to problem solving. Debrief the experience each time so that students become more aware of the strategies that helped them—or held them back.

Chapter 8

Gaming for Real Learning

Digital games may seem like an escape from learning, but that's not how innovative educators view this highly engaging medium. This chapter shows how teachers are leveraging student interest in gaming to develop projects with real-world implications.

On an otherwise ordinary day at Manual Arts Senior High School in South Los Angeles, flyers went up around campus offering free breakfast to anyone who could provide information about a lost "Pufftron." Details were sketchy. When twelfth graders walked into their English classroom later that day, they noticed a small electronic device with a grid of LED lights and a cartoonish image of a cloud. Could this be the mysterious Pufftron?

Teacher Antero Garcia—who was in on the mystery—quickly approved his students' request to claim the reward. Then for the next seven weeks, he guided them on an immersive learning experience called the Black Cloud that deliberately blurred the lines between "what was real and what was game."

The Pufftron, it turned out, was a wireless device that monitored local environmental quality, including several indicators of air, light, and noise pollution. Students were challenged to locate more Pufftrons hidden around their neighborhood, to interview people affected by pollution, and to make sense of the data being collected and reported in real time. Throughout the extended game play, they designed models for futuristic, sustainable ecotopias and made videos about environmental issues in their local neighborhood. They also advocated for practical, short-term ideas to enhance their predominately low-income community, including steps to improve the air quality in their own classroom. The Black Cloud culminated in a public event at a neighborhood art gallery where students used their enhanced communication skills to speak up about issues that matter to them. By playing a game, students discovered their own capacity to be change agents.

The potential of harnessing games for powerful cross-disciplinary learning is drawing attention from teachers, researchers, game makers, and even school designers. Some educators are simply looking for ways to engage students who spend much of their out-of-school time on gaming. Others see new potential for reaching learning goals, such as a network of teachers exploring strategies to use the popular multiplayer game World of Warcraft as the springboard for academic study. Physics teachers have flocked to Angry Birds as a vehicle for teaching about force and trajectory. Quest for Learning is a school model that uses gaming as the cornerstone of instruction.

Games like the Black Cloud set the stage for collaborative learning experiences that have real-world implications. It's an alternate reality game, which deliberately blurs the lines between the game world and the real world. Game designer Jane McGonigal, author of *Reality Is Broken*, explains the distinction: "First, alternate reality games are not in a virtual environment. They're built on top of social networks, so we use ordinary online tools like online video, blogs, wikis, and being part of a network. It's not about graphics and avatars. Second, it's real play and not role play. You don't adopt a fictional personality. You play as yourself."

McGonigal and her contemporaries tend to design games that focus on authentic global issues like oil dependency or poverty reduction. As she explains, "We want people to bring the same curiosity, wonder, and optimism that you feel in your favorite video games into your real lives and real problems."

How did Garcia, an English teacher, happen to bring his students into playing the Black Cloud, a game about environmental science? And how did playing the game help students, many of whom are learning English as a second language, develop their voice as writers and speakers? It's a story worth recounting, because it offers insights into how innovative teachers think—and act.

Garcia happens to be a frequent visitor to a Los Angeles storefront gallery called Machine Project. It's a neighborhood place known for edgy performance art and exhibits that often straddle the boundaries of art and science. "It's what you'd imagine if Bill Nye the Science Guy ran an art gallery," Garcia says. He attended one event called Tomato Quintet. Here's the artists' statement about that exhibit:

> The Tomato Quintet involved five pods filled with tomatoes. The pods were sealed from the outside world and contained sophisticated sensors which logged CO_2, light, and temperature changes inside the pods. The sensors

> recorded the ripening of the tomatoes over ten days. We
> compressed these data recordings in time to produce a
> 44-minute sonification of the entire ripening process. In
> the gallery, we played the music while serving pasta with
> tomato sauce made from the very tomatoes we recorded.
> (Niemeyer, n.d.)

That's not the whole story. The exhibit was, in part, a response to a recent tragedy in which refugees had tried to cross the border by hiding in a giant container of tomatoes. They were poisoned by the release of gases.

This multisensory art experience—plus the compelling backstory—grabbed Garcia's imagination. "I just thought, this is the coolest thing ever. I'm going to email whoever created this. I'd love to do something interesting about the environment in my classroom." He wasn't sure quite where he might be able to go with data-sensing devices, but he had some ideas.

He shot off an email to artist Greg Niemeyer, who is also a professor of new media at University of California, Berkeley. "I didn't really expect to hear back," Garcia admits, "but he responded a week later and asked if I was interested in applying for a grant together." They collaborated on a proposal for an extended inquiry project that was funded by the MacArthur Foundation's Digital Media and Learning Competition. The grant gave them resources they needed to unleash the Black Cloud at Manual Arts Senior High School, including a set of the portable Pufftron devices and a companion website that collected local environmental data in real time.

By connecting with an outside expert like Niemeyer, Garcia and his students gained access to technology that would otherwise not have been available to them. Students had to figure out what the measurements on the Pufftron devices meant and then share what they learned using texting or social media tools such as Twitter. That also meant they had a need to use their mobile devices—which are typically off-limits at school—to gather and communicate data in the role of citizen scientists. In many ways, playing the Black Cloud took them out of their usual routines at school and opened new opportunities for connected learning.

Garcia makes a habit of looking for learning opportunities that blur the edges of classroom and community. Interesting project ideas often emerge from his own passions, which range from art to music to games. When he's exploring the community on his own time, he keeps his eyes open for topics that might resonate with his students. He doesn't hesitate to "reach out to people from spaces outside of school. I've just gotten comfortable asking," he says. He also makes a habit of speaking up at community events where the voice of teachers and students is often missing. At a local forum about graffiti, for instance, he wondered aloud why there were no other educators in attendance. That got him involved in developing a new curriculum, which opened more opportunities to engage his students in their community.

Like many innovative educators, Garcia is also an avid learner himself. Doctoral studies at the University of California, Los Angeles have opened more opportunities to involve his students as coresearchers and copresenters about the projects they undertake together. A strong theme in his dissertation is *student agency*: "It's about giving students opportunities to take ownership over not only what they're learning, but also the direction they take in approaching that learning. As a researcher, I look at a problem and figure out how I'm going to use these kinds of research tools to solve that problem. When students are able to think in a systems-level way, they get to a much more complex, robust way of thinking. It involves a lot more trust on the side of teachers to make those kinds of things happen."

But the results he sees show why it's worth the effort. One project, for example, involved students in the design of a game about gathering community stories. On a meta level, the game involved teaching students to be researchers. Garcia asked them to identify the topics they wanted to explore through stories. Their answers: violence, trash, tagging, stereotypes, and the absence of love in the community. The last category "was something an outsider wouldn't have worded that way," he admits, but it authentically reflected a theme that students wanted to explore.

Finally, Garcia makes his own learning public by blogging at The American Crawl (www.theamericancrawl.com) and publishing about his experiences on other sites, such as the National Writing Project's *Digital Is* (http://digitalis.nwp.org).

Reengage Learners With Games

The practices that help Garcia innovate with his students in South Los Angeles recur in other classrooms where teachers are looking to take learning to new levels. Chad Sansing, for example, teaches middle school students who are at risk of being disconnected from school because of issues ranging from poor literacy skills to power struggles with adults to simple boredom. "We have some students who are underperforming because they know the 'game' of traditional school and they don't want to play it. School, for them, becomes a place of dragging their feet on the academic treadmill. We want to get them off the treadmill and get them able to walk places themselves," he explains. The small-school setting, Community Public Charter School in Charlottesville, Virginia, is intended to reengage at-risk students before high school through arts-infused, differentiated instruction.

For some of Sansing's students, gaming is the spark that reignites their interest in learning. Yet he also knows that games may not appeal to every learner. Recognizing the right fit requires building relationships with students and supporting their growth toward more self-directed learning. As he explains, "This school's about, how can I help you accomplish what you want to accomplish?" If students are keen to learn through games, Sansing challenges them to think about, "What is it you want to do? How can you demonstrate learning from it? What can you show, make, or do that demonstrates what you know?" One boy, for instance, rose to that challenge by using a game called Minecraft to create an exquisite model of the Parthenon, which he had obviously researched down to the last detail.

Like Garcia, Sansing follows the innovation strategy of keeping his eyes open for opportunities. "When you're in a place to do things differently, opportunities kind of present themselves. You see a news article, or read a bit of research, or see a cool game, and you bring it in. Kids who are interested will run with it. For kids who don't respond, you continue to do that until they find something." Thinking in this way "is really hard for teachers," he admits. He's had to relinquish his traditional role as the keeper of curriculum and learn to codesign learning experiences with his students. But he's getting more comfortable in this space. "When you have that entrepreneurial, innovative mindset, you're hungry for new things. In this environment, we get to try things out and see what sticks. The goal is to offer enough variety so that you reach each kid."

McGonigal, who happens to be the daughter of two educators, is one of those big thinkers who recognizes the potential for bringing authentic gaming experiences into the world of school. I caught up with her at the U.S. finals of the Imagine Cup, a Microsoft-sponsored event where teams of high school and college students compete to design games or software that address serious global issues related to the U.N. Millennium Development Goals.

Games level up learning by "provoking positive emotions. That's why we play them," McGonigal tells me. "They encourage curiosity, determination, grit in the face of problems." What's more, games are designed to give players "a sense of success, of mastery over a goal. These positive emotions activate us. When we have a positive, deeply felt experience with a subject matter or a challenge, it stays with us. That's why you see really long-lasting impact from games. Playing a game for as little as ninety seconds can change how you feel for twenty-four hours."

As an exercise in critical thinking, McGonigal suggests going beyond playing games for learning and involving students in game design. The process involves understanding how an entire system works, whether it's a local ecosystem or a global economic system. EVOKE, for example, is an alternate reality game that she designed in collaboration with the World Bank Institute. Billed as "a crash course in changing the world," it engages players in a series of missions in which they respond to global issues, such as food shortages or health pandemics. They gain points for developing their "superpowers" of collaboration and innovative problem solving. McGonigal's goal was not only to create an immersive gaming experience but also to activate players to take their good ideas into the real world and make a difference. As a result of EVOKE, more than fifty new social enterprises were launched in communities around the world. "I like to think of every game," she adds, "as a solution to a problem."

In much the same way, youth participating in the Imagine Cup are challenged to translate a real-world issue into a game system that could represent the complexities of that problem. A well-designed game, McGonigal says, "lets you interact with all aspects of a problem. There are problems in the world that need more engagement. Games offer a better way to engage people, to inspire hope. There's a chance here," she adds, "for an epic win."

Gaming: How to Get Started

Look for opportunities to engage students in games that offer connections to important, real-world learning goals. This may involve learning more about gaming yourself or drawing on colleagues' or students' expertise with gaming. Here are two ways to get started.

1. **Learn with colleagues**: EVOKE offers an example of a game
   with real-world applications and educational value (Johnson
   et al., 2010). For ten weeks during the first run of the game
   in 2010, players from around the world, ages thirteen and
   older, took part in the online simulation. They faced weekly
   challenges to invent and implement creative solutions to
   issues such as food security, disaster relief, and human rights.
   Teachers who brought their students into this online learning
   environment documented what they were learning on a wiki,
   where they shared ideas for curricular ties to social studies,
   language arts, and other core content. They also took part in
   conversations on platforms like *Teachers Teaching Teachers*, a
   weekly webcast. As word got out about this engaging learning
   experience, more teachers wanted to get involved. High
   demand from the education community led to the World Bank
   Institute reopening the game for school groups. When teachers
   team up with colleagues on projects like this, they set the
   stage for professional learning that parallels student learning.
   Everyone wins.

   Borrow from this example and build a professional learning
   network around a specific game that you think has learning
   value.

2. **Let students lead**: Teachers who are exploring gaming for
   learning acknowledge that students tend to be the experts
   when it comes to game mechanics and game strategy. You can
   leverage their know-how by facilitating projects that challenge
   students to design their own games. Encourage motivated
   students to enter youth game design competitions, such as the
   annual Game Changers Kids Competition or Imagine Cup.
   (See appendix A, page 135, for more details about these and
   other opportunities.)

Strategy Spotlight: Look for Crossroads

At a glance: Innovators deliberately work at the intersections of
disciplines. Radical collaboration leads to better ideas.

When to use this strategy: When framing problems or engaging with others

In a twist on interdisciplinary problem solving, the global gaming community recently rallied to solve a problem in ten days that has perplexed medical researchers for more than a decade. By playing a spatial reasoning game called Foldit, gamers helped scientists understand the protein structure of an enzyme that plays a critical role in how the HIV virus proliferates. This new understanding may help scientists develop anti-AIDS drugs. Foldit was developed at the University of Washington's Center for Game Science, where the focus is "to solve hard problems in science and education that currently cannot be solved by either people or computers alone," according to Zoran Popovic, director of the center (Gray, 2011). Results of the breakthrough were announced in a scientific journal, listing scientists and gamers as coauthors.

Interdisciplinary thinking is a strategy of innovators who avoid getting their thinking stuck in silos. By making a habit of what's known as radical collaboration, they combine divergent ideas into singular solutions. At Stanford's d.school, problem solvers from diverse fields follow these steps to radical collaboration: "We help each other even if it's inconvenient. We ask for help when we are stuck. And, we defer judgment long enough to build on each other's ideas" (d.school, n.d.b).

Online collaboration tools have dramatically expanded the opportunities for practicing grassroots teamwork, whether the task is editing Wikipedia, designing public spaces, or playing multiplayer games that have real-world implications.

Architecture for Humanity, through its Open Architecture Network, invites global collaborators to help design a better-built environment for the one in seven people around the world who live in slum conditions. This marathon design effort is not limited to professional architects. The Open Architecture Network makes a point of welcoming "designers of all persuasions," including community leaders, nonprofit groups, volunteer organizations, government agencies, technology partners, health care workers, educators, and others. These diverse experts come together online to share, comment on, and improve on each other's ideas, producing better designs than anyone could have developed alone. Such mass collaboration is intended to help the network achieve what it calls its "simple mission," of generating "not one idea but the hundreds of thousands of design ideas needed to improve living conditions for all."

In education, an interdisciplinary push is currently underway to promote the study of STEM (or STEAM, if arts are included along with science, technology, engineering, and math). Unless we build a talent pipeline in these fields, the worry is that we will be facing a near-term shortage of qualified employees and an innovation vacuum in scientific and technical fields.

A groundbreaking effort is underway in Cleveland, Ohio, to fill this pipeline with a more diverse population, including students who are passionate about visual arts. The eXpressions Art Program was started by the Cleveland Clinic, a center for medical care and research. Northern Ohio, like many parts of the United States, has shifted away from manufacturing. "Health care is the occupation of the day. And when you look at how unprepared students are in science and math," says Rosalind Strickland, who heads the clinic's Office of Civic Education Initiatives, "we know we have to find new ways to create this pipeline."

The eXpressions Art Program is a multifaceted effort that combines project-based learning for students, school-community collaboration, and professional development for teachers. It unfolds in several phases. First, there's a paid summer internship program in which students conduct original science research projects with mentoring from Cleveland Clinic doctors and researchers. Students present their projects, science-fair style, to medical experts and other community members. But that's just the first stage. When they return to high school in the fall, students also present their science research to art and writing classes, challenging their peers to use creative writing or visual arts to interpret their research for a broader audience. The results can be stunning, requiring creativity plus a thorough understanding of the science research they are interpreting. One student, for instance, fashioned an elaborate piece of wearable art to represent how the body responds to blood transfusions. "Art students may not start out feeling excited about science research," admits Strickland. "But we've found that students do get excited by science by approaching it through their passion. Science is no longer something they read about in a textbook. It's something they learn about from their peers and can connect to their own lives." Since 2005, nearly 600 alumni of the program have earned $23 million in college scholarships. Three are already in medical school, more than 100 are enrolled in premed programs, with still more pursuing careers in nursing, pharmacy, and other science-related fields.

"We're constantly looking to take this to the next level," Strickland says. "We want to take what we do inside the walls of the clinic, marry that with the education system, and bring real-world experiences into the classroom." By thinking across disciplines, she adds, "there's plenty of room for more innovation."

Borrow This Idea

How does change occur? This open-ended question was the spark for an interdisciplinary project for students at Metropolitan Arts & Tech High School in San Francisco, California. Students focused on a social revolution in history and explored the factors contributing to change through the lenses of artists, historians, and physicists. Then they represented their understanding by designing Rube Goldberg–like digital devices that tell an important story about how interrelated factors can lead to social upheaval. They presented personal essays and academic evidence to back up their claims. (Visit www.envisionprojects.org /cs/envision/view/env_p/193 to see examples of student work at the Envision Schools Project Exchange.)

Projects like this, as well as the eXpressions program described previously, offer ideal opportunities to invite experts in your community to provide authentic feedback to students. This takes planning. Use your network to locate people with experience in specific fields (don't overlook parents, professional organizations, colleges, and local businesses). Make the best use of experts' time by explaining in advance what kind of feedback you are seeking. Provide them with a template for organizing their comments.

Part III

Moving From Thinking to Doing

Bringing more innovation to your school or classroom requires a shift from thinking to doing. Part III focuses on taking action—a hallmark of innovators. First, we'll meet some educators who use their networks to help good ideas grow. In the last chapter, we'll suggest action steps that may be appropriate now or in the near future. Why such an emphasis on action? Let's trust the advice of legendary innovator Leonardo da Vinci: "I have been impressed with the urgency of doing. Knowing is not enough; we must apply. Being willing is not enough; we must do."

Chapter 9

Spreading Good Ideas

As we've heard throughout this book, innovators know how to take good ideas to scale. Their efforts may start small, but game-changing ideas need to engage a wide audience if they are going to take hold and make a lasting difference. In this chapter, we hear how educators use their professional networks to extend and improve upon effective strategies.

Mike Town, environmental science teacher at Redmond High School in Washington, remembers exactly where he was when he had the flash of inspiration that became the Cool School Challenge. He and his wife were riding bikes along a favorite trail. During the ride, Town was thinking about then-Seattle mayor Greg Nickel's green challenge to mayors across the country to reduce their city's carbon footprint by adopting the Kyoto Protocol locally.

"I kept wondering, 'How could I help?'" recalls Town, who has spent three decades working on environmental causes and twenty-five years in the classroom. He's also someone who has spent his life in small towns. Personal experience helps him frame the problem at the local level. "I know, from being a small-town person, that the single-biggest stationary greenhouse gas source in cities of 10,000 or less is the local high school. If a city wants to sign on to this challenge," he realized, "the first place they should be looking is their local high school." His excitement increased as he imagined bringing students into the equation. "It's STEM education. It's relevant. It would save districts money. What a win this could be!"

Town stopped his bike and started talking through the idea with his wife, a middle school science teacher. For the next hour, they brainstormed everything from what Kyoto-like protocols for schools might look like to where they could find support to take this bold idea to scale. Their friends later nicknamed the place on the trail where it all began as "the million-dollar spot."

It didn't take long for Town to find a range of community partners eager to support the idea so that teacher workshops and curriculum would be available for free. "Free is the only way to scale it up," he insists. With support from Puget Sound Clean Air Agency and others, he was able to develop a set of carbon-reduction protocols for schools, pilot test a curriculum, and launch a website. He rolled out the project with Redmond High students in spring 2007 and began hosting workshops for interested teachers from other schools. "From there, things kind of went viral," he says, including an invitation to present the idea to the U.S. Conference of Mayors.

Although Town's passion is what got this project started, he relies on measurable data to make the case for why it's a good idea. Through steps like turning off lights, turning down heat, recycling, and convincing teachers to carpool, Redmond High saves the district an estimated $40,000 annually on utility costs. The school's footprint has been trimmed by some 225,000 pounds of carbon dioxide. Through the project, students learn about environmental engineering, data analysis, and other topics that put STEM concepts to practical use. The project website tracks results from schools across the country that have collectively saved more than 2 million pounds of carbon (and that's only from schools that have registered—many more are unofficial participants).

The biggest surprise? "It's actually easy," Town says. "We say that we're teaching a new language, and that language is *Carbonese*. You learn that every action has a carbon consequence. Some are big, some are small. We want people to know that when you make decisions, the carbon consequence is quantifiable and has impact. You can lessen that impact very easily. Kids pick up on this quickly," he says. They also understand the multiplier effect of small savings being repeated across many locations.

The Cool School Challenge was recognized in 2008 with the President's Environmental Youth Award, earning Town's students a trip to the White House. In 2010, the project won the Green Award from the NEA Foundation. Town spent the 2010–11 school year as an Einstein Fellow at the National Science Board.

In many ways, the Cool School Challenge demonstrates what can happen when teacher innovation becomes a sustainable resource. Although Town appreciates the recognition, he is quick to point out that he is only one of many innovative teachers "who came up with an idea that has immense potential for scalability." He also recognizes that going from the spark of inspiration to the development of a scalable program is a serious challenge. "As a teacher, you have to make a choice. Either you leave the classroom to do the painstaking work of finding funding and doing workshops, or you take on a huge uncompensated burden," he says.

Town also chose to invest countless volunteer hours to bring the Cool School Challenge to life. "I know there are so many other teachers who have good ideas. But if they don't know how to develop it or they don't have the time, the idea just dies."

This isn't the only idea Town has helped to scale. He was also instrumental in obtaining state approval for a career and technical education course, Environmental Engineering and Sustainable Design. It's a project-based course in which students explore green jobs and develop solutions to environmental challenges. Projects help them understand important topics relating to alternative energy, water and waste management, transportation, urban and community design, and green construction. Students also develop expertise in specific career skills such as drafting, energy auditing, 2-D and 3-D design, GIS/GPS, and engineering testing. So far, at least twenty high schools in Washington State are teaching a version of this new course.

Perhaps even more importantly, Town adds, the hands-on course helps diverse students develop the confidence they need to tackle challenging academic work and see themselves as college material. That's something he understands personally. When he graduated from high school, he didn't even consider college. Instead, he worked as a machinist and in landscaping before eventually finding his way back to college—and a rewarding career in teaching. "One of the reasons I didn't go right into college was that I lacked confidence. I didn't take the right classes. I thought, 'I'm not smart enough. I'll fail.'"

As he considers the mounting STEM crisis and hears the nation's leaders searching for ways to build the pipeline for science and engineering, Town can't help but think about the students who share his background. If STEM initiatives focus only on attracting already high-achieving students, he worries, "We'll skim the elite students and overlook the kids who like to tinker." Yet when he looks at the solutions that are emerging from the Environmental Engineering and Sustainable Design course, he sees tangible evidence of good thinkers. "Some of these kids are geniuses who have been overlooked for years. Where are we going to find tomorrow's innovators? It's not always predictable who they're going to be."

Town's stealth strategy is to use the career and technical education class as a gateway for Advanced Placement Environmental Science. At Redmond High, about half the student body takes this popular course, and their pass rate on the challenging AP test is nearly 90 percent. When Town's nontraditional students score a passing AP grade, he uses the occasion to remind them about life's possibilities. "I say to them, look, you passed this test. It's not easy; across the U.S., half the kids who take it fail. What gives you the right for a second to think you're not capable of succeeding in college?"

Town's passion for his work is palpable, but he knows that passion alone won't solve the STEM crisis or launch a new generation of innovators. That's why he invests the extra effort to make sure good ideas take hold and grow, whether it's by connecting with interested partners or working through the regulatory system to get new course standards approved.

Use Networks for Innovation

By using personal learning networks and online communities, innovative educators are getting their ideas out into the world so that they can grow and be sustained by the energy of colleagues.

Bill Ferriter offers a good example. This teacher from North Carolina is passionate about a microlending project he started with his sixth graders (featured as an idea to borrow on page 50). Students use Kiva, the online microlending platform, to make small loans to entrepreneurs in the developing world. In the process, they gain new insights into core social studies concepts, such as understanding differences between the developed and developing world. Students also hone their analytic skills by digging into statistics about global poverty and evaluating entrepreneurs' business ideas. Once students select a borrower they want to support, they hone their powers of persuasion by making "pitches" to classmates about what makes a particular case compelling. The extensions for real-world learning are almost unlimited, as students apply their understanding of everything from math to international politics (Ferriter & Garry, 2010).

Ferriter started his school's Kiva Club after hearing a colleague mention microlending on Twitter. Right away, Ferriter saw the potential for engaging his students through authentic learning that would get them thinking—and acting—globally. Going from the spark of an idea to actual project meant doing research, gathering supporting materials, and piloting a new curriculum in the classroom. Determined not to keep this good stuff to himself, he has made his microlending toolkit available online (go.solution-tree.com/technology /reproducibles_TTiG.html). He also continues to blog about the idea, which inspires more good suggestions from other teachers. That's how good ideas not only travel but get better through collaboration. (Ferriter's blog post, "One Tweet CAN Change the World," describes the evolution of the lending club idea: http://teacherleaders.typepad .com/the_tempered_radical/2010/12/one-tweet-can-change-the-world .html.)

Shelly Blake-Plock and the Teach Paperless movement show how social media can take a good idea viral, leading in unanticipated directions. Blake-Plock, a high school teacher from Maryland, started blogging about his efforts to teach in a paperless classroom after his school went to 1:1 laptops. He mused publicly about interesting questions: How often do you start a class by asking students to take out paper and pencil? What if you decided to go paperless for a day, a week, or even longer—how would your teaching practices change? One post, "I Was a Paper Junkie," quickly went viral (Blake-Plock, 2009). Part of the appeal was his self-deprecating humor. But there was a bigger message in that post that resonated with other educators.

Via Twitter and the blogosphere, Blake-Plock launched the Teach Paperless challenge. He asked fellow educators to give up their attachment to paper for just one day, Earth Day 2010. By April, more than a thousand teachers around the world had signed on.

That was impressive, but even more so was how this one-day event grew into a movement. As Blake-Plock and others discovered, giving up paper also creates a reason to rethink and remodel some old-school teaching habits. Shifting to online workspaces such as Google Docs not only saves paper, but opens new opportunities for collaboration and just-in-time feedback. Having students post on blogs instead of in spiral-bound journals turns the solo reflection process into a conversation. Recording student brainstorming with a Web 2.0 tool like Wallwisher creates a more enduring—and shareable—artifact of student thinking than old-fashioned sticky notes. When these and more examples are captured in wikis and a Google Doc, ideas continue to expand.

After the success of the Earth Day pledge, many teachers were eager to keep going with paperless classrooms. In January 2011, *TeachPaperless* (http://teachpaperless.blogspot.com) became a collaboratively written blog "dedicated to conversation and commentary about the intertwined worlds of digital technology, new media, and education" (Blake-Plock, 2009). More than a conversation, it has become a grassroots innovation platform.

Help Good Ideas Go Viral

As you move forward with projects that encourage innovative thinking, share your experience so that others can learn with you, offer helpful feedback, and benefit from your reflections. Use your own blog, collaborative publishing sites, and tools like Twitter or other social networks to help your good ideas go viral.

Newton said it best: "If I have been able to see further than others, it is because I have stood on the shoulders of giants." Innovators have always made advances by building new ideas on existing platforms and products. Henry Ford may have brought us the first affordable automobile, but it took another innovator named Paul Galvin to popularize the car radio.

More recently, a flurry of innovation has followed the introduction of everything from personal computers to mobile devices. Innovators understand that they don't have to start from scratch. Instead, they can stand on others' shoulders to extend the reach of their ideas.

Writer Steve Johnson offers Twitter as a classic case of what's known as end-user innovation. What's significant, he says, is "the fact that many of its core features and applications have been developed by people who are not on the Twitter payroll" (Johnson, 2009). He's not just talking about the add-ons created by third-party developers. Twitter users themselves continue to invent new uses for the tool, whether it's for prodemocracy events in the Arab world or global charity drives like Twestival, which has raised nearly $2 million for good causes. Educators are part of this movement, too, using Twitter to connect for weekly edchats.

David Risher, a former executive with Amazon, was traveling abroad when he was inspired to build something new with existing tools. At an orphanage in Ecuador where his family had been volunteering, he noticed a building with a padlocked front door. It was the library. When he asked to look inside, the staff told him they had misplaced the key. After being read countless times, the dusty books stacked inside no longer held interest for the children living at the orphanage. Risher contrasted that story with the reading habits of his two daughters, who had been churning through books during their travels. The difference was that both girls had e-readers and could download any title that struck their fancy.

Risher has started a nonprofit called Worldreader to bring all the world's books to those in the developing world. His strategy is to use e-readers in rural villages to leapfrog print books and catalyze a new culture of reading. What makes the approach feasible, he says, is the reach of mobile networks into nearly every corner of the world. The same network that connects mobile phones is also used to download books. Worldreader is still in the early stages, but already it has spawned another new idea. With the introduction of e-readers, local publishers in far-flung places are recognizing new opportunities to digitize their book lists and sell titles online. That means new economic opportunity for publishers and authors, and also a way to make more native-language books available to students in the developing world.

Again and again, innovators show us how one good idea paves the way for more.

Borrow This Idea

TED began in 1984 as a conference celebrating good ideas in technology, entertainment, and design. It's become a global force for spreading worthy ideas, with two annual showcase events plus a video library of TED talks, a fellows program, and even a TED prize granting "one wish to change the world" each year.

In 2009, TED organizers took the bold move of inviting anyone—anywhere in the world—to host independently organized TEDx events, so long as they register and stick with a few ground rules. By giving away "the keys to the kingdom," as one blogger put it, TED has spawned conversations worldwide (Martin, 2012). By 2012, the tally was 12,900 TEDx talks in 129 countries.

Stand on the shoulders of TED and help organize a TEDx for your community. Independent events can be location-focused or have a more specific theme such as youth or education. In 2010, Conejo Valley School District in California put on the first TEDx event organized for an entire school district. The theme for the day was "What's the Big Idea," and explored three topics: thinking, doing, and seeing. Presenters included youth as well as adults from the community, discussing everything from effective communication to the neuroscience of belief. The audience also included mixed ages.

See www.ted.com for guidelines and more information about planning TEDx events.

Chapter 10

Taking Action

Here's an insight that innovators instinctively understand: doing something—however small—has a way of precipitating more action. When researchers looked at why some community-based initiatives failed while others thrived, they identified *taking action* as a key indicator of success (Dedrick, Gallivan, Mitchell, Moore, & Roberts, 1998). Even small-scale initiatives give people a sense of accomplishment and encourage them to persist. Without action, it turns out, nothing much happens.

Whenever I get the chance to interview innovators, I ask how they recommend getting promising ideas off the ground. There's a pattern to their often-humble advice: "Just begin." "Put one foot in front of the other." "Try something and see what happens next." Of course, taking an idea to implementation, and perhaps to a big scale, is a much longer, more complicated story. But it often starts with doable first steps.

When visiting schools that are taking deliberate action to encourage innovation, I'm often reminded of Edison's idea factory. In the Menlo Park, New Jersey, workshop where he perfected his design for the incandescent light bulb, Edison brought together an interdisciplinary collection of thinkers and doers. Along with engineers and chemists, his staff included a mathematician, glass blower, even a press team to spread the word about their breakthroughs. Edison's two-story workshop featured not only state-of-the-art equipment but also a pipe organ where employees could gather for sing-a-longs to refresh their spirits. Edison didn't just invent a better light bulb. He designed a whole system for generating and perfecting good ideas (Hof, Burrows, Hamm, Brady, & Rowley, 2004).

In *Where Good Ideas Come From*, author Steve Johnson (2010) reminds us, "Some environments squelch new ideas; some environments seem to breed them effortlessly" (p. 16).

Transforming school into an environment that effortlessly breeds ideas requires concerted action. As we've seen in the many preceding examples, innovative educators aren't waiting for the old system to

121

give way before they try new approaches. They're taking action now, within the constraints of standards and test scores, because they are determined to prepare students for the important work ahead of them.

There is every reason to believe that this focus on innovation will help students make gains on more academic measures. We've heard example after example about projects that have heightened student engagement, encouraged higher-order thinking, required the use of problem-solving strategies, and provided an authentic need for students to collaborate. The growing research base about project-based learning underscores the benefits of such projects to help students master important content and be able to apply their understanding to future problems (Darling-Hammond et al., 2008). Emphasizing innovation within the project-based learning framework means that students are also deepening their ability to frame problems; generate, evaluate, and improve ideas; and use teamwork and networking to go from idea to action.

This is the skill set that our students need for a successful future. That's why a school like the Henry Ford Academy-Dearborn—which has a cumulative graduation rate of more than 90 percent, with 100 percent of its graduating classes of 2007, 2008, and 2009 accepted to colleges and universities—is emphasizing innovation within the standards-based curriculum. That's why high-performing schools like Science Leadership Academy, which sent 97 percent of its graduates to college in 2010, give students room to learn from failure during the iterative process of problem solving.

Science Leadership Academy Principal Chris Lehmann says he frequently returns to this essential question: *how can we help our students innovate?* He elaborates: "How is school design related to that? The more walls we put up—physical walls and mental walls—the less we let students innovate. Classrooms should be lenses, not silos. You don't think in a silo. You don't think in a box."

To move ahead on the innovation front, schools are starting to take down some of those walls. Many of the following action steps suggest systems changes, which in turn will support the work of individual teachers. None are quick fixes. Creating an innovation culture requires a willingness to continue testing, fine-tuning, and improving on systems. That's how innovators operate.

Find Your Edge

Learning at the edge is a phrase I've encountered again and again while visiting schools that embrace innovation. They are willing to challenge old boundaries between school and community to forge something new at the intersection of institutions. "A key component of innovation," explains Deborah Parizek of the Henry Ford Learning Institute, "is that it happens at the edges of known areas."

Learning at the edge means challenging old boundaries between school and community, between academic subjects and real-world problems, between theory and action, between thinking and doing. Authentic projects offer opportunities to engage students in community issues and to work with outside experts. Internships, mentorships, and service-learning provide more experiences that connect students with the world beyond the classroom walls.

In *Education Nation*, Milton Chen explains why the George Lucas Educational Foundation, which he directed for a dozen years, seeks to showcase great teaching and learning that happens "on the edges" of traditional school systems. Like businesses that find new opportunities on the peripheries and at the boundaries of mature markets, schools also must look to the edges to find worthy new approaches. Yet these fresh ideas seldom get noticed—let alone emulated—by school systems determined to stick with the way we've always done things (Chen, 2010).

For too many students, any learning that feels "edgy" tends to happen outside the regular school day. Away from school, many students navigate virtual worlds and social networks. Some devote hours to online gaming, honing their skills as they evolve from novice to expert. Some 96 percent of nine- to seventeen-year-olds devote at least part of their out-of-school time to Web 2.0 culture (National School Board Association, 2007). Yet many schools continue to keep online spaces walled off from the school day. Students may be developing considerable expertise and passion during their outside-of-school activities, but this is seldom valued as "real" learning.

As the *2011 Horizon Report* for K–12 points out,

> Many activities related to learning and education take place outside the walls of the classroom and thus are not part of our learning metrics. Students can take advantage of learning material online, through games and programs they may have on systems at home, and through their extensive—and constantly available—social networks. The experiences that happen in and around these venues are difficult to tie back to the classroom, as they tend to happen serendipitously and in response to an immediate need for

knowledge, rather than being related to topics currently
being studied in school. (Johnson, Adams, & Haywood,
2011, p. 6)

Similar observations are offered by Mimi Ito, a cultural anthropologist who observes how youth engage with digital media and what they learn in the process. In *Hanging Out, Messing Around, and Geeking Out*, she and her research team describe how youth are actively learning and acquiring expertise through their use of digital tools and online spaces. Not only are kids going online to socialize and explore, but this is where they're gaining the technological skills and literacies they will need to succeed (Ito et al., 2010).

John Hagel III, a business strategist, and John Seely Brown, former director of the Xerox Palo Alto Research Center, suggest that we learn to pay better attention to the edges. As they predict, "The edges will reshape and eventually transform the core" (Hagel & Brown, 2005, pp. 10–11).

Action Step

Find your edge as a school or as a district. If your vision is to produce a new generation of innovators, figure out where you can be flexible enough to try some of the approaches you've heard about in the previous chapters. This may cause you and your colleagues to confront hard questions, such as:

- How tolerant is your community of out-of-the-box thinking?

- Does your school encourage suggestions from multiple stakeholders (including students)?

- Are you willing to challenge traditions if that will remove barriers to innovation?

- What will success look like?

Answering these questions will almost certainly require engaging with diverse audiences. To expand your thinking, put innovation strategies to work. Host a design challenge, borrowing the approach that helped the Henry Ford Learning Institute engage with diverse thinkers about its model for 21st century learning. Frame a particular issue or challenge that would benefit from fresh ideas, as Science Leadership Academy does with EduCon, and invite a wide range of community members—including students—to tackle it together. Put constraints on time the way engineers do when they get together for hackathons. If wild ideas emerge, be prepared for the next steps of evaluating, refining, prototyping, and, eventually, putting them into action.

Develop Common Processes

Changing from traditional teaching to an approach like project-based learning can be an uphill battle if you're the only one in the building making the switch to more authentic, student-centered instruction. Conversely, schools that adopt common processes make it easier for both students and teachers to adopt new ways of teaching and learning. That's been the case for schools that are part of the New Tech Network, the High Tech High charter schools, the Expeditionary Learning model, and others that have demonstrated success with project-based learning. These schools may not see student innovation happening in every project, but they consistently reinforce the 21st century skills that can lead to breakthrough thinking.

Similarly, Science Leadership Academy builds its innovation culture with core values of inquiry, research, collaboration, presentation, and reflection that carry across grade levels and disciplines. These values apply to teachers and administrators as well as to students. Every teacher, for example, plans projects using the same backward design approach, starting with the end in mind. Teachers grade student work using a common rubric. Teachers have dedicated time to collaborate, to be critical friends, and to reflect on students' work together. This school culture reinforces trying new ideas and innovating within this accepted approach to project design.

As we've heard, schools that are part of the Henry Ford Learning Institute use the signature Foundations of Innovation curriculum. This required course creates common learning experiences for all incoming students and equips them with a problem-solving approach that they can apply across disciplines. Schoolwide design challenges engage students in community problem solving. By their senior year, students are ready to tackle mastery experiences outside of school that enable them to put their innovation skills to work on real-world challenges.

Action Step

Build common processes that will enable teachers and students to move ahead with innovative projects. Schools that have invested time to develop these processes are likely to have:

- **Common planning time**—Dedicated time for collaboration allows teachers to design interdisciplinary projects and provide each other with critical feedback.

- **Common scoring guides**—Developing common language to assess 21st century skills like collaboration, critical thinking, and innovation means teachers (and students) are speaking the same language when they talk about quality work.

- **Common reflection time**—Dedicated professional time for reflection at the end of projects allows teachers to examine student work together and look for evidence of innovation.

- **Common networks**—Having systems in place to connect students with outside experts makes it easier to extend learning into the community.

Remove Barriers

Some teachers manage to innovate in spite of school cultures that limit their ability to try new ideas, but the effort can be wearing. A teacher in a large urban district, for instance, told me how he has to run interference with campus security whenever he sends students out of the classroom to do investigations. One project involved using mobile phones for data gathering, an activity he had cleared with his principal. Even though he pointed this out in lesson plans, he came back from an absence to find that his substitute had sent students to detention for using their phones during class. Such challenges "make it difficult to do this kind of work," he admits.

Getting barriers out of the way is equally important for teachers and for students. The goal should be helping students "get down to the work of learning more quickly. They need to be busy doing powerful work for themselves, not for us," insists Chris Lehmann. He barely pauses for breath when he warms up to this topic. "Then kids can innovate. Then they can get to project-based learning. Then they can see anything they're learning as a lens to view the world."

Action Step

Find out what teachers and students see as barriers to implementing innovative ideas, and then take steps to get these obstacles out of the way. For example:

- Survey students and teachers about current technology and social media policies. Do they have access to the tools necessary to innovate?

- Establish classroom practices that allow students to learn from failure. Build time for prototyping and making revisions into project schedules. Ask students to reflect on their processes for problem solving.

- When projects go well, provide opportunities for teachers and students to showcase and celebrate their innovative efforts.

- Allow safe spaces for staff to deconstruct "good failures," too. Keep in mind the advice from teacher Matt Van Kouwenberg: "Just don't fail the same way twice."

Find Allies at the Edges

Look for opportunities to connect with community allies who share your interest in student innovation.

In Gwinnett County, Georgia, the opening of a new high school with a 21st century career focus offered a chance to build alliances with local professionals focused on digital media, gaming, and other industries that thrive on innovation. Lanier High's Center for Design and Technology (CDAT) has an advisory board that includes a number of industry representatives. These advisers operate as a brain trust, opening their doors for field trips, providing feedback for students and teaching staff, and offering authentic assessment of student projects. They also offer a sounding board for creative teachers like Mike Reilly, who has developed the project-based, studio-style CDAT program with an eye for authentic learning.

"It's all about opportunities," Reilly tells me. In meetings with industry advisers, he can ask, "What's coming? What are the next big ideas? What do our students need to be ready for?" Advisers also play an important role as "connectors," introducing Reilly to others who can open doors for his students. He encourages other educators to "find a niche in your community. Start with one connection and build from there. You never know where it might lead." Recently, CDAT was awarded $40,000 as part of the Innovation Generation grant program from the Motorola Solutions Foundation to extend the school's model of real-world, project-based learning across the district.

Connecting students with mentors and internships offers opportunities to immerse them in innovative work environments. In Akron, Ohio, a city with a history of innovation as "the Rubber Capital of the World," middle schoolers from the National Inventors Hall of Fame School regularly work on innovation projects with an engineer-in-residence from Goodyear Tire. Such alliances are part of a regional effort to turn a brain drain into a talent network. Area businesses also open their doors to teachers, so that they can better understand the environments where their students will soon be heading (Henderson, 2011).

Action Step

Be creative about engaging with community allies. For example:

- Survey nonprofit organizations (especially those that have innovative community programs) about projects your students might take on, such as developing public service announcements or leading social media campaigns about causes students care about.

- Tap parent expertise. Find out about the skills of parents (and extended family members), and tap this expertise as a resource for student projects. Look for more than career skills. Parents may offer valuable insights about specific issues if they are "experts in a problem." Engage them for focus groups or user interviews, or to provide project feedback.

- Establish an innovation advisory council, including local industry representatives, nonprofit leaders, and university researchers or community college instructors.

Practice Innovative Teaching

We've heard about the value of rapid prototyping as a key strategy of engineering and design thinking. This process of creating prototypes that you can test and improve through feedback also belongs in every teacher's toolkit. When teachers are fine-tuning project plans, they can use rapid prototyping to invite feedback (from colleagues, outside experts, and students), make adjustments, and then see what happens during implementation. Projects will get better with each iteration if teachers make a habit of reflecting on what worked, what didn't, and how they can improve on the plan the next time around. When they approach curriculum design this way, they're modeling what it means to think and work like an innovator.

Action Step

Try your hand at innovative teaching with projects. For example:

- Build time for project review into your curriculum design process so that you invite feedback from colleagues before you implement project plans.

- Debrief projects, too, and include feedback from students. Use their insights to improve on the project the next time you use it.

Encourage Innovation in Informal Learning

What would students make or do if they had opportunities to innovate outside the regular school day? Starting an innovation club or Makers Club is one way to find out without the pressures of the traditional school day. Informal learning opportunities give students the chance to explore their interests and passions.

Learning that happens in out-of-school settings can ignite new ideas for the regular school day. Teacher Lucas Gillespie started a World of Warcraft Club for at-risk students at middle or high school levels. His idea was to use the wildly popular multiplayer game as a focal point for writing and literacy, mathematics, digital citizenship, online safety, and 21st century skills. After a successful first year, the club morphed into a language arts class with game-based content on the hero's journey theme. Meanwhile, Gillespie has been joined by a community of educators who share teaching strategies on the World of Warcraft in School wiki (http://wowinschool.pbworks.com).

Action Step

Help students pursue their interests and apply innovative thinking in afterschool clubs or other informal learning activities. Connect students with community programs that match their passions. For example, Girl Scouts of the USA has introduced a new set of badges that challenge girls to take the lead on innovation challenges.

Showcase Results

Foster a culture of innovation by showcasing what students can do when they put their innovation skills to work. Have students display their products in public spaces of the school or community, and include student statements about their work as part of the exhibit curation. If students are creating digital content, use the opportunity to publish it online and invite feedback. If students are entering competitions that challenge them to solve real-world problems, celebrate their efforts and invite local media to interview them about what they have accomplished. Let your community know that your students are actively engaged in creating and improving on ideas.

Action Step

Encourage students to take part in global events that put their problem-solving skills to good use. Imagine Cup, Intel International Science and Engineering Fair, and Ashoka's Activating Empathy competition are just a few examples. See appendix A (page 135) for more ideas.

Patience, Persistence, Potential

Breakthrough ideas often seem like overnight success stories, but that's seldom the case. Patience, persistence, and potential also play essential roles in the innovation process.

At an Intel International Science and Engineering Fair a few years back, I listened to two Nobel laureates describe for students what it feels like to have a great idea. Leon Lederman, a 1988 Nobel Laureate in physics, offered a tantalizing glimpse of the moment of discovery: "It usually happens at three in the morning. Suddenly, you become aware of a fact or a process that no one on the planet knows. You've learned something important. There are signs. Your palms sweat. You get chilled." The next step, he said, is deciding whom to awaken with a phone call. "Call someone important to you." The experience, he added, "may not happen often. Maybe once in your life. But it's unbeatable." Carl Wieman, a 2001 Nobel Laureate in physics, promptly added that such moments of discovery are indeed wonderful—but they're just the start. "Have the guts to pursue it, once you see you've discovered something new and different," he told students. "Have the courage and confidence to follow up."

Even if you begin with a good spark, an idea won't catch fire without follow up. Innovators understand the need to bring others on board to share, shape, and sustain an idea. When students, teachers, and others in a community combine their collective energies in support of worthy ideas, the results can be transformative.

Visit Miner County, South Dakota, today and you'll find a rural community busy reinventing itself for the 21st century. Innovation is what's powering this new future, and the hub for generating fresh ideas is the Rural Learning Center in Howard, South Dakota. The $6.5 million facility is a demonstration site for clean energy, complete with solar panels, a wind turbine, and geothermal heating. This offers an ideal setting to bring rural leaders together to share ideas about reinventing their communities. Miner County offers itself up as a learning laboratory for this grassroots innovation work.

None of this was imaginable twenty years ago when Randy Parry was a local high school teacher. Like many rural communities, Miner County was losing its most valuable resource: young people. As family farms failed, Parry watched his brightest students move away in search of better opportunities. They left behind an aging population and dwindling resources. "We knew we had a problem," Parry says.

To turn this dire situation around, Parry and others hatched an idea that catalyzed the whole community to learn at the edges. "We knocked down the walls of school and got people talking—young people and the elderly, business owners and ministers. Before that, everybody was operating in silos. They were all making decisions based on their concerns alone. We knew we could no longer continue to do what we had done in the past. We needed new pathways," he recalls. In a decision that would prove pivotal, high school students were charged with leading those conversations, which involved everything from discussing shared readings about rural America to researching the underlying causes of the county's struggles.

One of the action projects that helped ignite lasting change was led by students from Parry's vocational business class at Howard High School. Their project focused on local spending habits and was framed with a compelling driving question: *is your behavior killing your community?*

Students sought to find out how people's shopping habits affected the health of their community. They surveyed local business owners to determine where people spent their money and what factors shaped their spending decisions. They interviewed neighbors and parents to find out what motivated people to drive seventy miles to Sioux Falls, for instance, instead of buying locally. They applied their understanding of economics to estimate the impact if people would increase their local spending by just 10 percent. In a sparsely populated county, they estimated the 10-percent difference would be $7 million. In fact, when the idea grew into a yearlong spend-local campaign, the real impact turned out to be more than $15 million in gross revenue, which led to better funding for local services. Students continued spreading their message about the power of local spending at public events and around family dinner tables. They became change agents.

The Miner County Cash Flow Study has become somewhat legendary in community development circles. Authors Chip Heath and Dan

Heath, writing about the project in *Switch: How to Change Things When Change Is Hard* (2010), cite it as an example of how big problems can be addressed by breaking them into bite-sized pieces. To help other communities learn from its example, the Rural Learning Center has synthesized key lessons from the project into a report that's published on the center's website. Like other innovators, these forward-looking community members understand the importance of sharing good ideas.

The students' cash flow project turned out to be a critical first step in a long reinvention process for Miner County. Eventually, the county's community-building efforts attracted grant support, an influx of new investments, and development of the Rural Learning Center. Parry still stays in touch with many of the young people whose ideas helped invigorate the community. He doesn't have to look far to find them. Miner County sees more than 40 percent of its high school graduates return after college, nearly double the rate for rural communities. Several who were part of the cash flow study now serve in local leadership roles.

Miner County's story shows what can happen when students truly see themselves as innovators, able to come at problems with fresh ideas and use their passion to inspire others to join them. It's not hard to imagine similar stories unfolding in Detroit, Philadelphia, and the other places we've visited in these pages. By building learning cultures that encourage innovation, these communities are unlocking the capacity of students and teachers alike to envision—and then go create—a more vibrant future.

"You can be the one" are the words that teacher Michael Thornton uses to inspire his students to think like innovators. Who will be the ones to unleash innovation in your community?

Afterword

Researching this book has given me a chance to see innovation in action in schools across the United States. As I went about my scouting expedition, I noticed a pattern. Many of the teachers and school leaders I interviewed wanted to know where else I was visiting. They often asked: Who else is doing this kind of thing? And what are they learning?

Their questions suggest that we need to have a much bigger conversation about innovation in education. It's not enough for CEOs and politicians to say that innovation is an important goal. Figuring out how to prepare our students to innovate will require ideas from diverse thinkers, because no one has a corner on innovation. This conversation needs to start with a broad definition that includes social innovation and the arts along with the STEM fields. And it needs to put educators at the center. They are the ones who will bring the study of innovation to life as an engaging, empowering way to teach and learn.

As I said at the outset, the first step in teaching students to innovate is making sure educators have opportunities to be innovators themselves. Giving teachers room to innovate and supporting their efforts along the way are the best strategies to make sure that today's students have a chance to grow into their role as tomorrow's good thinkers and problem solvers.

Making room for innovation doesn't mean slighting the standards-based curriculum. The projects featured in these pages accomplish the dual goals of addressing important content *and* challenging students to solve authentic problems in creative ways. It's not an either-or choice.

Formal research is underway about some of the leading-edge instructional strategies featured here. Results will be important for making the case for approaches like children's engineering and design thinking, and I plan to keep tracking and sharing outcomes.

Meanwhile, I'm eager to hear from educators who are making an effort to bring innovation to school. How are you unlocking your students' creative potential? How do your students respond to the invitation to take their learning to the edge?

Additional Resources

Educators who want to infuse the curriculum with a focus on innovation can draw on a wide range of resources. The following resources provide additional information and, in some cases, classroom materials about the key ideas introduced in this book.

Design Thinking

Design Thinking for Educators—www.designthinkingfor educators.com

Design Thinking Toolkit for Educators, a free downloadable resource on this website, contains the process and methods of design, adapted specifically for the context of K–12 education. The toolkit was developed by IDEO, a global design firm, in collaboration with Riverdale Country School, an independent school in New York City.

Stanford d.school K–12 Laboratory Wiki—https://dschool.stanford.edu/groups/k12

The Hasso Plattner Institute of Design at Stanford University, also known as the d.school, has developed extensive resources to integrate design thinking into K–12 education. The K–12 Lab Wiki provides how-to information for teachers interested in using design thinking as a methodology for creative problem solving. The wiki includes an introduction to the design thinking philosophy along with curriculum resources and design challenges.

Studio H—www.studio-h.org

Studio H is a public high school design/build curriculum developed by Emily Pilloton and Matthew Miller of Project H Design, a non-profit design organization. The Studio H experience teaches students design sensibility, applied core subjects, and industry-relevant construction skills. The goal is to help students—especially those living in low-income, rural areas—develop the creative capital, critical thinking, and citizenship necessary for their own success and for the future of their communities. The website includes curriculum resources and a project blog.

Digital Gaming

Games for Change—www.gamesforchange.org
Games for Change is a nonprofit organization that works to encourage the development of digital games that offer social impact, leading to humanitarian or educational benefits.

Games for Learning Institute—http://g4li.org
Games for Learning Institute, based at New York University, is researching critical questions about the relationship between gaming and learning. Using a graphic novel format, the institute describes its history and research focus (http://g4li.org/about/g4history).

Imagine Cup—www.imaginecup.com
Imagine Cup, sponsored by Microsoft, is a global competition that challenges high school and college students to use technology to solve the world's toughest problems. Categories include digital gaming, software design, and mobile development.

Innovation and Invention

Buckminster Fuller Challenge—http://challenge.bfi.org
The Buckminster Fuller Challenge is an annual competition to fund the design and implementation of solutions that promise to solve the world's most pressing problems. The website includes background information about entries along with the Idea 1.0 Index, a searchable database of initiatives that need support or further development. Visitors can contact project leaders, leave constructive feedback, or connect with others who share their interests.

Design for the Other 90%—http://designother90.org
A project of the Smithsonian's Cooper-Hewitt, National Design Museum, Design for the Other 90% includes exhibitions about world-changing solutions along with an open-source network for engaging a global audience in collaborative problem solving. Online materials include the backstories of projects and inventions designed to improve the lives of those living in extreme poverty. The current exhibit, Design with the Other 90%: Cities, showcases sixty innovative projects for the one billion people currently living in urban slums and squatter settlements.

The Lemelson Center for the Study of Invention & Innovation—
http://invention.smithsonian.org/home
   Part of the Smithsonian Institution's National Museum of American History, the Lemelson Center for the Study of Invention & Innovation offers a range of online educational materials, including backstories about a wide range of inventions.

Maternova—http://maternova.net
   Maternova is a global innovation marketplace for ideas and tools to save the lives of mothers and newborns in the developing world. This U.S.-based social enterprise enables doctors, nurses, and midwives to track new ideas via an innovation index, offering a window on products and protocols at the research and development stage.

OnInnovation—http://oninnovation.com
   A project of the Henry Ford Museum, OnInnovation offers an online collection of interviews with innovators past and present. Featured interviews with contemporary thinkers include Pierre Omidyar, founder of eBay; Dean Kaman, inventor of the Segway; and Will Allen, champion of urban farming. Historical footage introduces students to problem solvers like Henry Ford, Rosa Parks, and Thomas Edison. The Innovation 101 curriculum, appropriate for formal and informal learning, uses multimedia resources to teach innovation processes and skills.

PopTech—http://poptech.org
   PopTech brings together a diverse global community of innovators to share insights and collaborate to create lasting change. The website features videos about breakthrough ideas, conference presentations, and updates about ongoing innovation projects.

TED—www.ted.com
   Annual TED conferences feature presentations by some of the world's best "thinkers and doers," from fields such as science, business, culture, and global problem solving. In addition to an online library of TED Talks from annual conferences, the site includes videos from independently organized TEDxTalks, including many youth speakers.

Project-Based Learning

Buck Institute for Education—www.bie.org
   This nonprofit organization promotes project-based learning to improve 21st century teaching and learning. The website includes an extensive project library, downloadable project resources such as

planning guides and rubrics, research, and tutorials for do-it-yourself professional development about project-based learning.

Edutopia—www.edutopia.org

Produced by the George Lucas Educational Foundation, *Edutopia* promotes effective K–12 learning by advocating for innovative, evidence-based strategies that prepare students to thrive in their future endeavors. Project-based learning is presented as a core strategy for effective learning, with an extensive library of videos, articles, blogs, and classroom-ready materials.

Reinventing Project-Based Learning—http://reinventingpbl.blog spot.com

This blog, based on *Reinventing Project-Based Learning: Your Field Guide to Real-World Projects in the Digital Age* (Krauss & Boss, 2007), shares additional project-based learning resources and project highlights. A downloadable resource catalogs technology tools to support essential learning goals in project-based learning.

Social Innovation

Ashoka—www.ashoka.org

In keeping with its tagline of "everyone a changemaker," Ashoka has been a leader in identifying and supporting social entrepreneurs around the world. This website provides a searchable database of Ashoka Fellows, including background pages that describe each fellow's new idea and the problem it is designed to solve. Online competitions engage people from around the world in problem solving, such as a recent contest called Activating Empathy: Transforming Schools to Teach What Matters (www.changemakers.com/empathy).

The New Heroes—www.pbs.org/opb/thenewheroes

This four-hour documentary series from PBS introduces social entrepreneurs from around the world who are tackling poverty, illiteracy, food scarcity, and other global challenges with creative, sustainable solutions. This website includes companion material for the classroom.

Skoll Foundation—www.skollfoundation.org

The Skoll Foundation aims to drive large-scale change by investing in and connecting the social entrepreneurs and innovators who then work to solve the world's most pressing problems. The website includes profiles of eighty-five Skoll Fellows who are implementing their game-changing ideas on five continents.

Youth Venture—www.genv.net
A project of Ashoka, Youth Venture encourages a global community of young changemakers by supporting the work of teens who are tackling problems with sustainable solutions. This website describes an application process through which teens can qualify for funding for their ventures.

Innovation Rubric

This sample rubric suggests language for assessing specific innovation skills. The three skills included here—think creatively, work creatively with others, and implement ideas—are based on the Framework for 21st Century Skills (Partnership for 21st Century Skills, 2009).

Beginning	Developing	Proficient
Think Creatively		
Suggests obvious or previously attempted solutions	Can think beyond conventional or previously tried solutions	Uses multiple strategies to generate original ideas
Defers to others in brainstorming process	Learns to build on others' ideas	Can lead others in brainstorming
Demonstrates limited ability to express thinking	Can make visual representations of thinking (such as sketches)	Can represent thinking in various forms so that others can understand and respond to ideas (such as sketches, prototypes, or storyboards)
Shows limited ability to test ideas or invite feedback	Shows ability to prototype, test, and evaluate ideas	Can use iterative process to prototype, test, evaluate, elicit feedback, and synthesize to improve on ideas
Gives up when ideas don't work or are not well received by others	May be frustrated by failed attempts	Can learn from failure (one's own and others') and document process to improve future results

continued →

Beginning	Developing	Proficient
Work Creatively With Others		
Listens to others' ideas and suggestions Contributes to team effort when asked	Shares ideas and offers useful feedback to team members Is open-minded Shows responsibility to team effort	Actively contributes original ideas and feedback to team Amplifies others' thinking and models how to build on good ideas Shows leadership in helping advance team effort
Implement Ideas		
May be frustrated by challenges or setbacks Shows limited ability to plan action steps Learns to manage time effectively	Understands how to meet goals with manageable steps Shows some persistence in face of setbacks	Can manage project timeline and envision and successfully respond to potential challenges Able to advocate for solutions and garner support from others

Discussion Guide

Bringing Innovation to School describes innovation as a process that is both powerful and teachable. Discussions with colleagues will help educators deepen their understanding of innovation and consider how they might equip students with a new set of skills to tackle 21st century challenges. This guide is intended to encourage productive conversations about the challenges and opportunities of teaching innovation.

Part I: Setting the Stage

Chapter 1: Coming to Terms With Innovation

1. Chapter 1 begins with several famous quotes about innovation. Which comes closest to your current understanding of this term?

2. John Kao describes innovation as an evolving concept with four historical stages. What role do you imagine your students playing in shaping the next stage of innovation? What new skills will they need to think innovatively and put ideas into action?

3. This chapter describes the efforts of several social innovators. Are you familiar with social innovators who are working to improve your community or solve a problem that you care about? What makes their problem-solving approaches innovative?

4. In discussing the creative strengths measured by the Torrance Test, the author suggests that these behaviors—being energetic, talkative, unconventional, humorous, and lively or passionate—might be labeled as disruptive in traditional classrooms. Do you agree? Discuss specific strategies you have used to encourage student creativity. What results have you seen?

Chapter 2: Seeing Educators as Innovators

1. This chapter suggests that the first step in teaching students to innovate is making sure that educators have opportunities to be innovators themselves. Do you consider yourself an innovator? Describe something you have done that demonstrates one or more of the traits of innovators as outlined in this chapter.

2. How has the culture of school encouraged you to innovate or limited your ability to try new ideas in the classroom?

Chapter 3: Growing a New Global Skill Set

1. This chapter outlines a problem-solving process that innovators use. Where in this process do you see natural connections to the classroom? For example, a language arts teacher might see "refining ideas" as closely connected to how students improve their writing through peer editing and revision. What other connections do you notice?

2. In the story about Dots in Blue Water, teacher Michael Baer explains how he designed a project around a student's question. How might you incorporate more student voice into the design of inquiry projects?

3. Discuss the "smart team" qualities that researchers have identified (such as being open minded and sharing criticism constructively). How do you teach, model, or encourage these teamwork skills? How do you build a classroom culture that reinforces effective collaboration?

4. Several empathy-building activities are described in this chapter. Which of these seem appropriate for your classroom? What other activities do you use to encourage students to consider issues from multiple perspectives?

Part II: Building the New Idea Factory

Chapter 4: Seeding Innovation

1. This chapter describes several action research projects underway in Albemarle County Public Schools. If you had funding available to investigate a research question, what

would you propose? Who would be your ideal collaborators for an action research project?

2. District administrator Becky Fisher emphasizes the importance of "growing the seeds" of innovation projects. What processes does your learning community have in place to evaluate action research and disseminate effective ideas? How does your school culture encourage educators to learn from small mistakes so they are not repeated?

Chapter 5: Integrating Design Thinking Throughout the Curriculum

1. This chapter describes how the design thinking process is being used within the standards-based curriculum. Discuss how you might remodel a traditional unit so that it is framed as a design challenge. How might design thinking lead students to acquire deeper content knowledge or proficiency with 21st century skills?

2. Immersive professional development experiences give teachers opportunities to learn about design thinking by doing it. What would motivate you to learn more about design thinking? What would you need to know before introducing this process to students?

Chapter 6: Making Room for Thinkers

1. This chapter describes a "tinkering studio" elective offered at St. Gregory School in which the process of innovating is as important as the final product. How might you assess student work in this context? What would you expect students to know, produce, or be able to do as a result of their self-directed learning experience?

2. Two strategies are offered for creating more flexible learning opportunities: (1) find room in the physical space of school or (2) find room in the schedule. Discuss these options. What are the challenges and opportunities of each, given your context?

Chapter 7: Taking Advantage of Technology

1. This chapter introduces an emerging technology—the tabletop digital fabricator—that is being introduced to

elementary schools as part of a children's engineering curriculum. Discuss the potential benefits for students being able to rapidly produce physical models of their ideas (or as Glen Bull puts it, "to see their concepts make the trip from an initial conceptual idea to a final physical form"). What do you do now to help students make their thinking visible?

2. Teacher Paula White describes engineering as "a process for solving problems and a language to explain thinking." Do you agree with her statement that teaching children about engineering fits naturally into the elementary curriculum? Discuss how this approach might lead to deeper understanding of core math and science concepts.

Chapter 8: Gaming for Real Learning

1. This chapter describes what students accomplished by playing an alternate reality game called the Black Cloud, in which they analyzed real-time data about pollution in their neighborhood. Game play also involved conducting interviews, making videos about local environmental issues, and advocating for practical solutions. How do these activities—connected to standards in a high school English class—challenge your understanding of gaming?

2. For middle school teacher Chad Sansing, games offer just one possible hook to engage learners who are at risk of disconnecting from school. He acknowledges that designing high-interest projects *with* students requires him to relinquish control over the curriculum. "This is really hard for teachers," he says, but is a necessary part of developing an innovative mindset as a teacher. What do you think of his comments?

Strategy Spotlights

Part II introduces five innovation strategies: (1) be opportunistic, (2) think in metaphors, (3) take time to explore, (4) learn to fail, (5) look for crossroads.

1. Which strategies seem most suited to teaching and learning? Discuss how you might introduce one or more of these strategies during a project to inspire or motivate students.

2. The strategy of learning from failure has been cited throughout this book as a way that innovators frequently work. In education, however, failure has negative connotations that may be difficult to overcome. How might you create safe opportunities for students to take intellectual risks, learn from mistakes, and improve their work through revision? Discuss changes that may be needed in formative assessment, project timelines, student reflections, peer review, or grading practices to encourage a "fail safe" environment for learning.

Part III: Moving From Thinking to Doing

Chapter 9: Spreading Good Ideas

1. Mike Town, the teacher who developed the successful Cool School Challenge, acknowledges the difficulty of turning the spark of an idea for the classroom into a sustainable model. Discuss the barriers that keep you from acting on innovative ideas. What kind of support would help you move ideas forward?

2. This chapter includes examples of teachers who expanded on innovative ideas through their professional networks. How do you make use of your professional network now? How do you use social media for collaboration? Discuss situations in which your network has helped you improve on an idea.

Chapter 10: Taking Action

1. This chapter suggests seven action steps to move forward with an innovation agenda. Do you agree with the author's observation that innovators often begin with small, doable first steps? Which step (or steps) do you feel ready to take now?

2. Discuss the phrase "learning at the edge." What does this expression mean to you when you think about your context for teaching and learning? Can you identify potential allies at the edge of your school and community to enlist in an innovation agenda?

3. What ideas from this book will you bring into your work in education? How will your students benefit from what you have learned?

References and Resources

Alleyne, R. (2010, October 5). 'Mucking about' with pencil lead and sticky tape wins Nobel prize for physics. *The Telegraph.* Accessed at www.telegraph.co.uk/science/science-news/8043657/Mucking -about-with-pencil-lead-and-sticky-tape-wins-Nobel-Prize-for -Physics.html on September 26, 2011.

Allison, P. (Producer). (2010, June 2). Visualizing information and envisioning new schools–TTT 203–06.02.10 [Audio podcast]. Accessed at http://teachersteachingteachers.org/?p=260 on September 26, 2011.

American Museum of Natural History. (2011). *Aidan: The secret of the Fibonacci sequence in trees.* Accessed at www.amnh.org/national center/youngnaturalistawards/2011/aidan.html on September 25, 2011.

Barseghian, T. (2010). *Design thinking: Creative ways to solve problems.* Accessed at www.edutopia.org/classroom-design-k12-laboratory on September 25, 2011.

Bell, L. (2011, June 6). *Curry takes engineering projects into local engineering classrooms.* Accessed at http://curry.virginia.edu/articles/curry -takes-engineering-projects-into-local-elementary-classrooms on January 11, 2012.

Benyus, J. (2002). *Biomimicry: Innovation inspired by nature.* New York: Harper Perennial.

Blake-Plock, S. (2009, April 30). I was a paper junkie [Web log post]. Accessed at http://teachpaperless.blogspot.com/2009/04/i-was -paper-junkie.html on September 25, 2011.

Bornstein, D. (2004). *How to change the world: Social entrepreneurs and the power of new ideas.* New York: Oxford University Press.

Boss, S. (2010, February 1). Jane McGonigal on gaming for good [Web log post]. Accessed at www.worldchanging.com/archives/010949 .html on September 25, 2011.

Boutelle, C. (2011). *Preventable hospital deaths can be reduced by encouraging error reporting.* Accessed at www.siop.org/Media/News/deaths .aspx on September 25, 2011.

Brilliant, L., & Brilliant, G. (2007). Aravind: Partner and social science innovator. *MIT Innovations, 2*(4), 50–52. Accessed at www.mit pressjournals.org/doi/pdf/10.1162/itgg.2007.2.4.50 on September 26, 2011.

Britannica Editors. (2010, October 18). The decline of creativity in the United States: 5 questions for educational psychologist Kyung Hee Kim [Web log post]. Accessed at www.britannica.com /blogs/2010/10/the-decline-of-creativity-in-the-united-states -5-questions-for-educational-psychologist-kyung-hee-kim/ on September 26, 2011.

Bronson, P., & Merryman, A. (2010, July 10). The creativity crisis. *Newsweek.* Accessed at www.newsweek.com/2010/07/10/the -creativity-crisis.html on September 25, 2011.

Bull, G., & Groves, J. (2009). The democratization of production. *Learning and Leading With Technology, 37*(3), 36–37.

Carr, A. (2010). *The most important leadership quality for CEOs? Creativity.* Accessed at www.fastcompany.com/1648943/creativity -the-most-important-leadership-quality-for-ceos-study on September 25, 2011.

Case, J. (2010, May 4). The painful acknowledgment of coming up short [Web log post]. Accessed at www.casefoundation.org/blog /painful-acknowledgement-coming-short on September 25, 2011.

Chambers, A. (2009, November 24). Africa's not-so-magic roundabout. *The Guardian.* Accessed at www.guardian.co.uk/comment isfree/2009/nov/24/africa-charity-water-pumps-roundabouts on September 25, 2011.

Chen, M. (2010). *Education nation: Six leading edges of innovation in our schools.* San Francisco: Jossey-Bass.

Christensen, C. M., Horn, M. B., & Johnson, C. W. (2011). *Disrupting class: How disruptive innovation will change the way the world learns.* New York: McGraw-Hill.

Darling-Hammond, L., Barron, B., Pearson, P. D., Schoenfeld, A. H., Stage, E. K., Zimmerman, T. D., et al. (2008). *Powerful learning: What we know about teaching for understanding.* San Francisco: Jossey-Bass.

Dedrick, A., Gallivan, M., Mitchell, G., Moore, N., & Roberts, S. (1998). *Listen and learn II.* Edmonton, Alberta, Canada: Author.

d.school. (n.d.a). *K12 laboratory: Learning spaces that embody design thinking.* Accessed at http://dschool.stanford.edu/k12/space.php on September 25, 2011.

d.school. (n.d.b). *Our point of view: Innovators, not innovations.* Accessed at http://dschool.stanford.edu/our-point-of-view/ on September 25, 2011.

d.school. (2010). *Bootcamp bootleg.* Stanford, CA: Hasso Plattner Institute of Design at Stanford. Accessed at http://dschool.typepad.com/files/bootcampbootleg2010v2slim-1.pdf on September 25, 2011.

Edmondson, A. C. (2011). Strategies for learning from failure. *Harvard Business Review.* Accessed at http://hbr.org/2011/04/strategies-for-learning-from-failure/ar/1 on September 25, 2011.

Encore. (2008). *Jock Brandis.* Accessed at www.encore.org/jock-brandis on September 25, 2011.

Ferriter, W. M., & Garry, A. (2010). *Teaching the iGeneration: 5 easy ways to introduce essential skills with web 2.0 tools.* Bloomington, IN: Solution Tree Press.

Florida, R. (2002). *Rise of the creative class: And how it's transforming work, leisure, community and everyday life.* New York: Basic Books.

Gershenfeld, N. (2006, February). *Neil Gershenfeld on fab labs* [Video file]. Accessed at www.ted.com/talks/neil_gershenfeld_on_fab_labs.html on September 25, 2011.

Gooding, J., & Metz, B. (2007). Inquiry by design briefs. *Science Scope, 31*(3), 35–39. Accessed at http://hub.mspnet.org/media/data/ArticleInquiry_by_Design_Briefs.pdf?media_000000005632.pdf on January 11, 2012.

Goodman, G., & Simon, K. (Directors). (2010). Frank Gehry [Television series episode]. In L. Arison (Executive Producer), *Masterclass*. New York: Simon & Goodman Picture.

Gray, L. (2011, September 19). Gamers succeed where scientists fail. *UW Today*. Accessed at www.washington.edu/news/articles/gamers-succeed-where-scientists-fail on September 27, 2011.

Hagel, J., & Brown, J. S. (2005). *The only sustainable edge: Why business strategy depends on productive friction and dynamic specialization*. Cambridge, MA: Harvard Business School Press.

Hamm, S. (2007, August 30). Radical collaboration: Lessons from IBM's innovation factory. *Bloomberg Businessweek*. Accessed at www.businessweek.com/innovate/content/aug2007/id20070830_258824.htm on September 26, 2011.

Heath, C., & Heath, D. (2010). *Switch: How to change things when change is hard*. New York: Broadway Books.

Heatwole, A. R. (2010, July 27). How to: Roll your own FailFaire [Web log post]. Accessed at http://failfaire.org/2010/07/29/how-to-roll-your-own-failfaire/ on September 25, 2011.

Henderson, F. (2011). *Businesses buy into STEM*. Accessed at www.hivelocitymedia.com/features/STEM6_2_11.aspx on September 26, 2011.

Herro, A. (2011, April 1). Fellows Friday with Apurv Mishra [Web log post]. Accessed at http://blog.ted.com/2011/04/01/fellows-friday-with-apurv-mishra/ on January 24, 2012.

Hlubinka, M. (2011, May 17). New models for education: Maker Faire and the Young Makers Program [Web log post]. Accessed at www.edutopia.org/blog/education-maker-faire-young-makers-program on September 25, 2011.

Hof, R. D. (2004, October 11). Building an idea factory. *Bloomberg Businessweek*. Accessed at www.businessweek.com/magazine/content/04_41/b3903462.htm on September 26, 2011.

Howe School of Technology Management. (n.d.). *What is the front end of innovation (FEI), the so called "fuzzy front end" (FFE)?* Accessed at www.frontendinnovation.com/ on September 26, 2011.

Hurd, B. (Director). (2010). *Full length interview with Dean Kamem* [Video file]. Accessed at www.oninnovation.com/topics/detail .aspx?playlist=1911&title=Dean%20Kamen on September 26, 2011.

Innovator Factor Foundation. (2010). *Innovation*. Accessed at http:// iffglobal.org/seoia.html on September 26, 2011.

Institute of Brilliant Failure. (2011). *Nobel prize by playing with pencil and Scotch tape*. Accessed at www.briljantemislukkingen.nl/EN /failures/failure/nobel-prize-by-playing-with-pencil-and-scotch -tape/ on September 26, 2011.

Intel. (2009). *Innovator factor foundation: An Intel international science and engineering fair (Intel ISEF) alumni case study*. Santa Clara, CA: Author. Accessed at http://download.intel.com/education/isef /profiles/ISEF_CaseStudy.pdf on September 26, 2011.

Iske, P. (2011, April). *TEDxMaastricht: Paul Iske: Brilliant failures in healthcare* [Video file]. Accessed at http://tedxtalks.ted.com/video /TEDxMaastricht-Paul-Iske-Brilli on September 26, 2011.

Ito, M., Baumer, S., Bittani, M., Boyd, D., Cody, R., Herr-Stephenson, B., et al. (2010). *Hanging out, messing around, and geeking out: Kids living and learning with new media*. Cambridge, MA: MIT Press.

J Lab. (2010). *Knight-Batten 2010 winners*. Accessed at www.j-lab.org /projects/knight-batten-awards-for-innovations-in-journalism /2010 on September 26, 2011.

Jenkins, K. (2006). *Confronting the challenges of participatory culture: Media education for the 21st century*. Chicago: MacArthur Foundation.

Johnson, L., Adams, S., & Haywood, K. (2011). *The NMC horizon report: 2011 K–12 edition*. Austin, TX: The New Media Consortium. Accessed at www.nmc.org/pdf/2011-Horizon-Report-K12 .pdf on September 26, 2011.

Johnson, L., Smith, R., Levine, A., & Haywood, K. (2010). *The 2010 horizon report: K–12 edition*. Austin, TX: The New Media Consortium. Accessed at www.nmc.org/pdf/2010-Horizon -Report-K12.pdf on September 26, 2011.

Johnson, S. (2009, June 5). How Twitter will change the way we live. *Time Magazine.* Accessed at www.time.com/time/printout /0,8816,1902604,00.html on September 26, 2011.

Johnson, S. (2010). *Where good ideas come from: The natural history of innovation.* New York: Riverhead.

Kao, J. (2007). *Innovation nation: How America is losing its innovation edge, why it matters, and what we can do to get it back.* New York: Free Press.

Katehi, L., Pearson, G., & Feder, M. (Eds.). (2009). *Engineering in K–12 education: Understanding the status and improving the prospects.* Washington, DC: National Academies Press. Accessed at http:// books.nap.edu/catalog.php?record_id=12635 on September 26, 2011.

Lahiri, M., Tantipathananandh, C., Warungu, R., Rubenstein, D., & Berger-Wolf, T. (2011, April). *Biometric animal databases from field photographs: Identification of individual zebra in the wild.* Paper presented at 2011 ACM International Conference on Multimedia Retrieval, Trento, Italy. Accessed at http://compbio.cs.uic .edu/~mayank/papers/LahiriEtal_ZebraID11.pdf on September 26, 2011.

Leadbeater, C. (2008, March 8). People power transforms the web in the next online revolution. *The Observer.* Accessed at www .guardian.co.uk/technology/2008/mar/09/internet.web20 on September 26, 2011.

Lehrer, J. (2012, January 30). Groupthink: The brainstorm-ing myth. *The New Yorker.* Accessed at www.newyorker.com /reporting/2012/01/30/120130fa_fact_lehrer? on April 1, 2012.

Maker Faire. (2011). *So you want to make a Maker Faire?* Accessed at http://makerfaire.com/mini on September 26, 2011.

Markham, T. (2010, September 12). The 21st century dilemma: Can we teach creativity? [Web log post] Accessed at www.thommarkham .com/blog/default/the-21st-century-dilemma-can-we-teach -creativity/ on September 27, 2011.

Marks, P. (2011, July 5). Robo-worm to wriggle through rubble to quake survivors [Video file]. *New Scientist.* Accessed at www.new

scientist.com/article/dn20654-roboworm-to-wriggle-through -rubble-to-quake-survivors.html on September 26, 2011.

Martin, C. (2012, March 9). A platform worth spreading [Web log post]. Acccessed at www.ssireview.org/blog/entry/a_platform _worth_spreading on Apri 1, 2012.

Martin, J. (2011, June 15). Designing the giant trike: New video from design-build tech innovation class [Video file]. *21k12*. Accessed at http://21k12blog.net/2011/06/15/designing-the -giant-trike-new-video-from-design-build-tech-innovation -class/#more-3622 on September 26, 2011.

Mianecki, J. (2011, June 15). Carry-all for homeless wins design competition [Web log post]. Accessed at http://blogs.smithsonianmag.com /aroundthemall/2011/06/carry-all-for-homeless-wins-design -competition/ on September 26, 2011.

Mullen, W. (2011, May 22). UIC scientists crack code on tracking zebras. *Chicago Tribune*. Accessed at http://articles.chicagotribune .com/2011-05-22/news/ct-talk-zebra-barcode-0523-20110522_1 _zebras-bar-code-animals on September 26, 2011.

National School Board Association. (2007). *Creating and connecting: Research and guidelines on online social—and educational—networking*. Alexandria, VA: Author.

Navarro, J. (2010, July 9). Playing with metaphors: Teaching is like . . . [Web log post]. Accessed at http://firesidelearning.ning.com /forum/topics/playing-with-metaphors on September 26, 2011.

Niemeyer, G. (n.d.). *Artwork 1996–2008: Open source art and new media by Greg Niemeyer*. Accessed at http://studio.berkeley.edu/niemeyer /art.html on September 26, 2011.

Noschese, F. (2011, July 27). The tower [Web log post]. Accessed at http://fnoschese.wordpress.com/2011/07/27/the-tower/ on September 26, 2011.

Nussbaum, B. (2011). *Design thinking is a failed experiment. So what's next?* Accessed at www.fastcodesign.com/1663558/design-thinking -is-a-failed-experiment-so-whats-next on September 26, 2011.

Partnership for 21st Century Skills. (2009). *P21 framework defini-tions.* Accessed at www.p21.org/documents/P21_Framework _Definitions.pdf on September 26, 2011.

Product Arts. (n.d.). *The fuzzy front end—Unfuzzied.* Accessed at www .product-arts.com/articlelink/461-the-fuzzy-front-end-unfuzzied on September 25, 2011.

Robert Wood Johnson Foundation. (2007). *Recess rules.* Princeton, NJ: Author. Accessed at www.rwjf.org/files/research/sports4kids recessreport.pdf on September 26, 2011.

Rojas-Burke, J. (2011, April 7). Legacy Health in Portland decreases infection rates, saving lives and money. *The Oregonian.* Accessed at www.oregonlive.com/health/index.ssf/2011/04/legacy_health _in_portland_beat.html on September 26, 2011.

Rosenberg, T. (2010, December 17). Spreading the care [Web log post]. Accessed at http://opinionator.blogs.nytimes.com/2010/12/17 /spreading-the-care/?ref=mali on September 26, 2011.

Saraf, D. (2009, July 13). India's indigenous genius: Jugaad. *Wall Street Journal.* Accessed at http://online.wsj.com/article /SB124745880685131765.html on September 26, 2011.

Scanlon, J. (2008, June 11). Peter Senge's necessary revolution. *Bloomberg Businessweek.* Accessed at www.businessweek.com/innovate /content/jun2008/id20080611_566195.htm on September 26, 2011.

Seidel, S. S. (2009). Remixing education: Hip hop pedagogy, school design and leadership. *Unboxed, 1*(4). Accessed at www.hightechhigh .org/unboxed/issue4/remixing_education/ on September 26, 2011.

Sharklet Technologies. (2010). *Technology: Inspired by nature.* Accessed at www.sharklet.com/technology/ on September 26, 2011.

Smith, K., & Petersen, J. (2011). *Supporting and scaling change: Lessons from the first round of the investing in innovation (i3) program.* Boston: Bellwether Education Partners. Accessed at http://bellwether education.org/wp-content/uploads/2011/07/Supporting-Scaling -Change-i3.pdf on September 26, 2011.

Snyder, G. (2011, February 10). Heroes for humanity: Using the sci-ence of behavior analysis to change the way the world works. *PM eZine.* Accessed at http://pmezine.com/Heroes-for-Humanity on September 26, 2011.

Turckes, S., & Kahl, M. (2011). *What schools can learn from Google, IDEO, and Pixar.* Accessed at www.fastcodesign.com/1664735 /what-schools-can-learn-from-google-ideo-and-pixar on September 25, 2011.

White, P. (2010, June 12). Time to explore passions in school? [Web log post] Accessed at http://coopcatalyst.wordpress.com/2010/06/12 /time-to-explore-passions-in-school/ on September 26, 2011.

Woolley, A., & Malone, T. (2011, June). Define your research: What makes a team smarter? More women. *Harvard Business Review.* Accessed at http://hbr.org/2011/06/defend-your-research-what -makes-a-team-smarter-more-women/ar/1 on September 26, 2011.

World Challenge. (2011). *Greenhouses on supermarket rooftops set to eliminate food miles and improve quality.* Accessed at www .theworldchallenge.co.uk/down_to_business/news/read/52 /Greenhouses_on_supermarket_rooftops_set_to_eliminate_food _miles_and_improve_quality on September 26, 2011.

Wright, S. (2011, December 13). Life in an inquiry driven, technol- ogy embedded, connected classroom: English [Web log post]. Accessed at http://shelleywright.wordpress.com/2011/12/13 /life-in-an-inquiry-driven-technology-embedded-connected -classroom-english/ on January 10, 2012.

Yamada, L. (2011). *Design thinking inspires Hawaii educators, indus- try leaders.* Accessed at www.kitv.com/news/28852012/detail .html#ixzz1XqfBkTlS on September 26, 2011.

Zhao, Y. (2009). *Catching up or leading the way: American education in the age of globalization.* Alexandria, VA: Association for Supervision and Curriculum Development.

Zhao, Y. (2011, July 17). Ditch testing (Part 5): Testing has not improved education despite all the costs [Web log post]. Accessed at http://zhaolearning.com/2011/07/17/ditch-testing-part-5 -testing-has-not-improved-education-despite-all-the-costs/ on September 26, 2011.

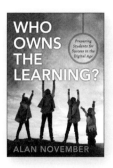

Who Owns the Learning?
Alan November
Discover how technology allows students to take ownership of their learning, create and share learning tools, and participate in meaningful work.
BKF437

21st Century Skills
Edited by James A. Bellanca and Ron Brandt
Education luminaries reveal why 21st century skills are necessary, which skills are most important, and how to help schools include them in curriculum and instruction.
BKF389

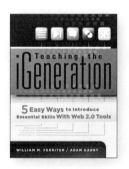

Teaching the iGeneration
William M. Ferriter and Adam Garry
Find the natural overlap between the work you already believe in and the digital tools that define tomorrow's learning.
BKF393

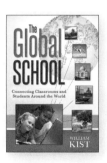

The Global School
William Kist
Wrapped in a 21st century skills framework, this book offers specific steps to globalize your classroom and strategies to encourage higher-order thinking.
BKF570

Solution Tree | Press

a division of
Solution Tree

Visit solution-tree.com or call 800.733.6786 to order.